THY KINGDOM COME

THY WILL BE DONE,
ON EARTH AS IT IS IN HEAVEN

MOSES E. KING

INTRODUCTION BY DR. DOUG BEACHAM

Moses E. King
3197 Preacher Henry Road
Faison, NC 28341

ISBN Number 978-0-578-05506-0

Printed by
LifeSprings Resources
P.O. Box 9
Franklin Springs, GA 30639

ACKNOWLEDGEMENTS

I would like to acknowledge the encouragement and support of Dr. Doug Beacham, and also thank him for his personal contributions to this work of love. I would like to thank the staff at LifeSprings for their refinement and assistance with preparing the script for print. I also owe a special thank-you to my secretary, Sally Bass, for always making time to assist me when needed. Finally, I want to thank my wife Dean for her encouragement and assistance with getting pictures together to accent the story.

Be Blessed!

Moses E. King

DEDICATION

It is with a grateful heart that I dedicate this book to my precious wife Dean, our son Moses Gregg, and our two deceased daughters:

Deborah Dean, October 20, 1960 – September 21, 1966
and
Janet Carol, December 19, 1967 – January 18, 1981

I am also proud to dedicate this book to two new generations of King Family Believers, our two grandsons, Scott and Spencer, and our three great-grandchildren, Chase, Raven, and Adison. These wonderful children are a real blessing to us in our maturing years.

FOREWORD

By Moses E. King

Throughout the past two thousand years, the Holy Spirit has been the active custodian of the Christian faithful. During some of this period of church history, the faithful have been only a remnant, while in other periods the gospel has produced great growth.

One such period of growth, which began in the seventeenth century, was evidenced in the ministry of John Wesley in England. The Wesleyan revival led to the formation of the Methodist Church in England and later in the American colonies.

In 1785, sent by John Wesley, the Rev. Francis Asbury came to the Goshen community of eastern North Carolina. Through his anointed ministry, the holy fire of revival came to this community.

Over two centuries later, as that truth continued to be preached in Methodist, Holiness, and Pentecostal Holiness congregations, the ground was prepared for the testimonies shared in this book. It is through that heritage that today financial and prayer support for Kingdom ministries continues around the globe.

This is the story of my father, Rev. Henry C. King (Preacher Henry), and what his life taught us as his descendants. Preacher Henry taught us that God would bless hard work and that God's Kingdom on this earth requires both hard work and financial resources.

This is also a story about you and me. I have come to understand the truth in God's Word that we are all "kings and priests" in the body of Christ. Our "kingship" relationship with Christ's Kingdom on earth provides great opportunity for all believers to find their maximum fulfillment in Christ. In Revelation 1:6, Scripture affirms that Jesus will present all of us to the Father as "kings and priests." This truth thrills me, and I pray that it will thrill you! We, then, are all "kings and priests," after the order of Jesus Christ, who redeemed us.

I have often reflected on the role of Melchizedek, who is introduced in Genesis 14:18 and referenced again in Psalm 110:4. This godly figure from the Old Testament is further described in the New Testament in Hebrews 5, 6, and 7. This "Christ-figure" in the Old Testament was also both the "King of Salem" and "Priest of the Most High God." Abraham, called and blessed by God, paid tithes to Melchizedek, thus affirming Abraham's commitment to God and independence from the spirit of the world.

The third section of this book provides more of what the Holy Spirit has spoken to me about "kings and priests" and "Melchizedek."

Why I Chose to Write "Thy Kingdom Come"

While traveling in 2010 to Eastern Europe with IPHC World Missions Ministries, I spent the night in a hotel in Budapest, Hungary. I was awakened early the next morning, filled with excitement as the Holy Spirit seemed to fill the room with His gentle presence.

As I meditated on God and His gracious provisions that allowed my family to be involved in Kingdom building around the world, I felt compelled to write down this title, "Thy Kingdom Come," together with some other facts about God's wonderful grace.

I was reminded also of these two Bible verses displayed on my office wall in North Carolina. These verses have been constant reminders to me of Kingdom principles:

"Except the Lord build the house, they labor in vain that build it: except the Lord keep the city, the watchman waketh but in vain." (Psalm 127:1)

"And God is able to make all grace abound toward you; that ye, always having all sufficiency in all things, may abound to every good work." (2 Corinthians 9:8)

These verses are for all Kingdom-minded people, especially the laity of the church. We must remember that we laity make up at least ninety-nine percent of the church!

The primary gifting of the "kings" (my view of the laity) is in the domain of helps and financial development of Kingdom ministries. Without the "kings," God's Kingdom on earth cannot expand and evangelize the world. We are all "kings and priests" through Jesus Christ; it is imperative that we discover and walk in the sphere of kingdom authority "the King, Jesus," has given us!

It is my prayer that multitudes of lay people will be encouraged as they realize their gifting as kings in God's Kingdom on earth. When our natural efforts and abilities are joined by God's supernatural ability, the results often confound the mind of man. As you read this story, may you be able to identify your own special giftings as "kings and priests" and be launched into your most rewarding years of Kingdom building! May we join our hearts and our resources together and continue to pray, "Thy Kingdom come" on earth, as it is in Heaven. Amen.

INTRODUCTION

By Doug Beacham

A dear friend of the International Pentecostal Holiness Church, Dr. Mark Rutland, once told me, "Doug, you never know when the next phone call will change your life."

That insight was never truer than a day in March 2006 in a hotel room in Kuala Lumpur, Malaysia. I was eight months into my first year as executive director of IPHC World Missions Ministries. The call came from my office and told me that Rev. Danny Nelson, the Missions director for the North Carolina Conference, had a layman who wanted to give a million dollars to World Missions Ministries. Rev. Nelson had asked the office to give him a date when I could come to eastern North Carolina and meet this businessman.

My response to the office was, "What time does he want me there!" Obviously this was exciting to all of us in World Missions, as we had been praying for a financial breakthrough of this magnitude.

I was on the front end of a nearly three-week trip to Asia with missions coordinator Russell Board. I made plans to complete my assignment in Asia, return home to Oklahoma City for one night to get fresh clothes, and make my way to a Piggly Wiggly grocery store in Mount Olive, North Carolina. I was joined by Dr. Harold Dalton, assistant director of World Missions Ministries, and Rev. Nelson.

We arrived at the busy, clean, and inviting grocery store for lunch with Moses and Dean King. In the small upstairs office of the store, I could hardly enjoy the tasty food as I listened to the amazing story of "Preacher Henry." I found myself humbled as I realized that this early IPHC missionary to Africa had found his place as both a "king and priest" in Christ's Kingdom and had poured his missionary spirit into the life of his son and daughter-in-law.

Moses and Dean King made the first-million dollar gift to the IPHC through the IPHC Foundation. It was earmarked primarily for the annual interest to construct churches in Africa. IPHC missionaries, such as the late Johnny Brooks and Philip List Sr., had inspired the King family.

Moses joined me on several overseas mission trips over a six-year period. These included ministry in Romania and Hungary (with then-Presiding Bishop James D. Leggett) and ministry in Myanmar and Malaysia (with then-Presiding Bishop Ronald Carpenter, Sr.). We also had special trips to the Ukraine and to Hong Kong. In both areas Moses King met with IPHC leaders such as Donavan Ng and Valeriy Reshetinskiy who fully understood the spiritual principles elucidated in this book.

Moses and Dean were present for the IPHC World Conference in Vancouver, where they continued to present significant checks to World Missions for special needs around the globe. Their gifts have been a great blessing to Holmes Bible College and local congregations in the United States. This has been in addition to the Foundation gift, which continues to bear fruit every year.

The passion of their life is contagious! One of their grandsons and his wife, Scott and Brandi King, are already involved in making mission trips with the IPHC.

My wife and I have learned so much from this wonderful husband and wife. They have taught us kingdom principles and expanded our faith. They are more than a precious gift to the IPHC; they are examples and mentors to us for what it means to walk by faith.

Moses has often told me that he prays that this book will inspire the "kings," the laity of the IPHC, to see the eternal value of their resources through the IPHC Foundation (www.iphc.org/iphfoundation). I heartily agree with him that this book will accomplish that goal.

On behalf of the global IPHC family, I offer my sincere thanks to this family and to our Lord Jesus Christ for what this family is doing to make a world of difference.

Doug Beacham was the executive director of IPHC World Missions Ministries from 2005 to July 2012. In July 2012 he became the general superintendent of the International Pentecostal Holiness Church, serving as the presiding bishop.

TABLE OF CONTENTS

SECTION
1

Preacher Henry

Rev. Henry C. King – "Preacher Henry"

SECTION 1

Preacher Henry

This amazing story begins on July 4, 1885, in the pine forest and plowed fields of the area known as "Suttontown" in eastern North Carolina's Sampson County. The cluster of families that lived there resided halfway between the small villages of Mount Olive and Newton Grove.[1]

Though the Civil War had ended twenty years earlier, rural communities like Suttontown had many living Confederate Army veterans as well as former slaves. Nearly every resident had at least one relative with a story of serving in the American Civil War. As for the women and children remaining in eastern North Carolina during the war, stories abounded of hiding food from General Sherman's Army while it raided most of the towns and villages north and east of Fayetteville in the winter and spring of 1865. These accounts became legendary and were vividly remembered for generations. The stories of former slaves became part of the unique history of eastern North Carolina blacks.

In the relatively short time that had elapsed since the surrender of the Confederate States, the slow process of national and local healing had already begun. The area remembered antebellum aspects of its life. Sampson County sent men to fight against the British in the Revolutionary War and the War of 1812. One of its citizens, Micajah Autry, fought in the War of 1812 and was one of the celebrated heroes who died with Davy Crockett in 1836 at the Alamo. They remembered William Rufus King (1786-1853), the thirteenth vice president of the United States, who served with President Franklin Pierce. King had the misfortune of being the shortest-serving vice president in United States history, having died of tuberculosis only forty-five days after taking the oath of office.

On this particular Independence Day in 1885, while citizens celebrated the birth of the blood-stained nation, there was another celebration occurring in the modest, but well-kept farmhouse of Joseph B. and Susan E. King. In

---

1. Editor's note: The first part of this narrative, since it is primarily historical, is written in the third person. Later in this chapter, and in the following chapters, the narrative shifts to include the first-person singular and plural with "I, we," and these are the words of Mr. Moses King referring to his experiences and memories.

the front bedroom, the cry of a newborn son announced the arrival of Henry Cleveland King, the sixth child born to the young couple.

Though Henry King was born into a Methodist family, they were like many of their day: nominal followers of John Wesley's brand of holy living. Even so, a little exposure to divine truth can bear unexpected fruit. By the late 1890s, Henry was drawn to a deeper personal consecration, desiring to be separated from the vices and allurements of the world.

Henry King grew up in a time when Methodism was experiencing a crisis over holiness. This turmoil had been brewing for several decades across the United States. It was believed that the main focus of the historic church had drifted away from its Wesleyan emphasis on holiness accompanied by clean living.

Consequently, holiness revivals swept across churches and communities and often led to separation between former members of traditional Methodist congregations. Henry and his sister, Clyda, were spiritually moved by these holiness revivals and became part of a new church in the Suttontown community, the Goshen Holiness Church.

In 1896, one of these holiness revivals swept through Sampson and neighboring counties. It was originally led by A. B. Crumpler from Clinton, North Carolina. Crumpler, whose preaching style and emphasis on holiness led many to seek sanctification at altars, impacted the lives of men like G. F. Taylor, A. H. Butler, and G. B. Cashwell, all of whom were leaders in the early days of the Pentecostal Holiness Church.

Henry not only responded to the personal call to salvation and sanctification, but he also responded to the Holy Spirit's call for him to enter into public ministry as a preacher in this new movement. It is hard for us to imagine today the cross that early Pentecostal Holiness pastors and parishioners had to carry. There was a strong social stigma against holiness people, which was expressed with pejorative terms like *holy-rollers* and *fanatics*. Though marginalized by society, friends, and family, these dedicated men and women walked passionately and faithfully in the steps of Jesus.

In addition to incurring the status of social outcasts, they also faced major decisions related to basic commerce and economy. The Holiness people recognized the moral and physical detriment of tobacco. Like social prophets, ahead of their time by nearly seventy years, they warned against using tobacco products. In order for such a warning to have integrity, those who sounded it were required to make decisions about growing and producing a product they knew to be harmful to the human body, even if it meant sacrificing the profits that came along with one of the biggest cash crops in the state.

Thus, the use and production of tobacco became a hot-button issue all across the South. While most farmers in eastern North Carolina grew cotton, corn, and vegetables, tobacco remained the primary crop. Most men enjoyed smoking and chewing tobacco, and many women enjoyed dipping snuff.

As a young man, Henry loved to smoke cigarettes. According to his personal testimony, he stopped smoking three times; and three times he went back to the habit. He struggled with the Apostle Paul's observation, "I find then a law, that, when I would do good, evil is present with me. For I delight in the law of God after the inward man: But I see another law in my members, warring against the law of my mind, and bringing me into captivity to the law of sin which is in my members. O wretched man that I am! Who shall deliver me from the body of this death?" (Romans 7:21-24, KJV).

As he wept, the Holy Spirit whispered into his spirit and said, "You have nothing to weep for. Look up and praise God!"

In the midst of this spiritual crisis, Henry went to the altar at the Goshen Holiness Church. Broken in spirit because he failed to keep his own good intentions, his weakness and the call to follow God drove him to cry out, "Lord, I have quit smoking three times and I can't do this alone. You will have to handle this desire for tobacco for me, if I am to be a clean vessel for your service." As he wept, the Holy Spirit whispered into his spirit and said, "You have nothing to weep for. Look up and praise God!" As he raised his head in response to the prompting of the Holy Spirit, profound joy washed over his soul. From that moment on, he was delivered from tobacco and never wanted another cigarette again. His life became a testimony to the delivering power of God to break addictions.

This single experience shaped Henry C. King's life in ways that few other events ever would. He was berated by his family and marked as foolish and radical. He suffered public ridicule and mockery because his personal conviction that using tobacco was wrong also meant that it was wrong for him to grow something he knew was physically and spiritually harmful for others.

Henry King was disparaged not only for what many considered being legalistic and holding radical views of holiness, but also on a greater level, he was scorned for rejecting the basic money crop that everyone assumed was necessary to make a living. If God called Henry to stop growing a major crop, how would God provide in its absence?

The fledgling holiness congregations met for their annual convention in Fayetteville, N.C., in 1904. There, they adopted the official position that laymen in the church were forbidden to use tobacco, and anyone who grew or sold tobacco could not hold membership in the church. Thus, Henry King was one of many who made life-changing decisions built on their understanding of holiness, the Bible, and a character shaped in the image of Jesus Christ.

From 1896-1906, the cluster of Holiness churches in eastern North Carolina faced and overcame the usual problems besetting an emerging movement: personality conflicts, theological differences, and financial strains. By 1906, many in the movement were longing for a fresh move of God. Many began to read about the Azusa Street revival in Los Angeles, California, that began in April 1906. The reports of Pentecostal tongues, healings, conversions, renewed holiness, and missionary efforts stirred the hearts of people like Henry King.

As Henry read these reports, then later heard them first-hand from men like G. B. Cashwell and others who received the Pentecostal baptism with speaking in other tongues, he found himself desiring to receive the gift of the Spirit. This supernatural empowerment ignited an inner desire to be a missionary. The Lord had impressed upon him a call to serve in Liberia, a West African country on the Atlantic Coast that had a large population of native Africans and African-Americans who had gone there to have their own nation.

It is important to remember that the preceding three years had led to major changes in the movement. Azusa Street Pentecost, with speaking tongues as the initial evidence of the baptism in the Holy Spirit, had profoundly impacted most pastors and laity. The change was so great that by 1908, A. B. Crumpler, the founder of the movement, resigned in protest of the Azusa Street teaching and returned to the Methodist church in nearby Clinton. The young churches had also caught the missionary spirit of Azusa Street and had already sent T. J. McIntosh to China. The movement had its own foreign missions board. J. H. King, a leader in the Fire-Baptized Holiness Church who was well-known among most holiness people in eastern North Carolina, left in 1910 for an around-the-world mission experience that changed his life.

It is important to remember that Henry King, in his middle twenties, was being influenced by these mighty men and women of God. He attended the Falcon Camp Meeting, where people like J. H. King, G. B. Cashwell, A. B. Crumpler, A. H. Butler, J. A. Culbreth, Sister Florence Goff, and G. F. Taylor, were faithfully preaching and living the full gospel of Jesus Christ. Sister Goff later would often visit the King home in the summer and join with the ladies in making her beloved pepper relish! These godly men and women mentored and helped disciple Henry King along with the saints in the Goshen Pentecostal Holiness Church. Their effectiveness remains a witness to us today![2]

It was during this time that Henry met and fell in love with a beautiful young lady named Donnie Jennette Eldridge. She was from a fine family of landholders. She was a born-again Christian and enthusiastically supported Henry's call to the mission field. By 1910, Henry was prepared to submit his call to the North Carolina Conference of the Pentecostal Holiness Church.

When the small denomination met for its annual convention in 1910, the twenty-five-year-old Henry King stepped into an assembly that had already made major changes and was shifting its thinking more globally. It was a historic convention in that it approved a motion for the Pentecostal Holiness Church of North Carolina to merge with the Fire-Baptized Holiness Church. The two groups formally merged on January 31, 1911, in Falcon, North Carolina, producing the structure and theological framework of what is now the International Pentecostal Holiness Church.

After Brother King's statement, the Holy Ghost set His seal of approval upon it in a miraculous way through the interpretation of tongues, giving messages of encouragement and comfort, which were unmistakable in their assurances.

Whether he realized it or not, Henry King was involved in something much larger than his own sense of call to Liberia. The Eleventh Annual Convention of the small movement met November 22-24, 1910, in the Holiness Tabernacle in Kinston, North Carolina. The official Minutes record that Rev. J. A. Marshburn, pastor of the Goshen Church, was present for the meeting that confirmed the young Henry as a missionary.

During the morning of November 24, Rev. H. C. King informed the conference of his call to Liberia as a missionary. The Minutes record:

> Bro. H. C. King, having felt called of God as a missionary to Africa, was requested to speak concerning his call and the leadings of the Spirit in that direction.

> After Brother King's statement, the Holy Ghost set His seal of approval upon it in a miraculous way through the interpretation of tongues, giving messages of encouragement and comfort, which were unmistakable in their assurances.

2. An excellent survey of these early years is found in Dr. Daniel Rollins, *Forward, Ever Forward: A History of the North Carolina Conference of the Pentecostal Holiness Church* (Franklin Springs, GA: LifeSprings Resources, 2011).

> By motion, Bro. King was acknowledged as a worthy
> missionary and the Convention pledged him its support.
>
> A collection was taken for missions and there was
> contributed $16.55.[3]

This inspiring record reads like a twentieth-century version of Acts 13:1-3, where Paul and Barnabas were called and commissioned for the First Missionary Journey. The same dynamic of the Holy Spirit was present among this band of Spirit-filled people who gathered in Kinston.

Henry King placed himself under the guidance and training of Rev. G. F. Taylor at the Falcon School in preparation for that ministry. At that time, because the denomination was so young, there was no formal missions program in place in the Pentecostal Holiness Church. Henry received the blessings of the church and prepared to provide his own support for the work to which he felt called. He planned to go alone and establish a place of reasonable safety, and then return to North Carolina and marry Donnie Eldridge. They would return and labor together in Liberia and the surrounding countries of West Africa.

In late 1911, Henry C. King made his way to New York by train and boarded a ship to Cape Town, South Africa. From there he traveled to Liberia and joined a missionary couple who had been sponsored by another denomination. This allowed him to push ahead and establish his own beachhead for the gospel in Liberia, and then prepare a place for his bride. All seemed to be going according to plan until illness struck the young missionary.

Preacher Henry was a kindly man with soft, blue eyes and a light skin tone. Therefore, the tropics proved to be physically hard on this devout man of God. He enjoyed much success with the gospel because many of the Liberians spoke and understood some English. Others spoke only in their native dialect, but God was faithful to honor Henry's efforts to bring the light of the gospel to this dark region of the world.

After several months of fighting mosquitoes and baking in the African sun, Henry's stamina began to wane. It was first thought that he was just pushing himself too hard, but after a while, the facts began to speak for themselves. Young Henry, as healthy and vigorous as he was, had contracted blackwater fever. Most white-skinned Englishmen did not survive this complication that arose from multiple attacks of malaria. Henry's English friends convinced him that he must seek medical treatment back in the United States if he were to survive. In 1912 Henry's friends assisted him in procuring a place on a ship to America. Upon arriving home, and with proper treatment and rest, he regained his strength.

---

3. "Minutes of the Pentecostal Holiness Church of North Carolina, Kinston, North Carolina."

Following this, Henry knew that physically he would not be able to return to Liberia with his new bride. He perceived God's wisdom that the Lord's vineyards were everywhere. He learned that when one door closed, God would faithfully open another. He discovered that even our disappointments serve His purpose.

Where would his open door be? What was God up to?

Soon Henry, his young wife, and their firstborn daughter, Dorcas, moved to Gastonia, North Carolina, for a two-year assignment as pastor of a congregation. Financially trying, this was indeed a labor of love, as pastors during this time received very little monetary support from congregations. Still, wisdom spoke again in clear tones. Pastoral assignment was fulfilling to the young couple, so they decided to move back to the farm and provide for their enlarging family, serving congregations as God opened doors.

They must have wondered what God was up to. They were once again being planted right in the middle of their families, surrounded by the world's way of thinking and shallow devotion to spiritual things.

They must have wondered what God was up to. They were once again being planted right in the middle of their families, surrounded by the world's way of thinking and shallow devotion to spiritual things. What were the Lord's purposes for their lives, as well as the lives of their "seed" that would follow?

BACK IN SAMPSON COUNTY

On September 1, 1916, Preacher Henry (as he had come to be called) and Donnie welcomed a second baby girl with great joy. They named her Ruth Elizabeth King. Things were becoming more stable for this young couple, and Preacher Henry had put together what looked like a genius operating model for a family farm.

Preacher Henry had dairy cattle to provide milk and butter for the family, as well as beef cattle for sale. He had hogs for the family smokehouse at hog-killing time, as well as slaughter hogs to sell. Donnie had chickens in the henhouse, which provided fryers and eggs for the family. There were always eggs left over to sell or trade for household necessities that the family farm did not provide. They even grew corn for feeding the livestock.

As far as crops were concerned, Preacher Henry grew cotton, sweet potatoes, bell peppers, cucumbers, squash, and a variety of beans. These items were transported by train in iced, cooled boxcars to wholesale markets in Philadelphia, Baltimore, Detroit, and Chicago. The family also had a personal garden abounding with fresh produce to enjoy in season, with enough left over for canning.

It would seem the only thing the King family's farm lacked was tobacco. But Preacher Henry had made a covenant with God, who had delivered him from cigarettes many years prior. He walked in the Light that God revealed to him.

In addition to farming, Preacher Henry pastored churches. He often drove as far as 25 or 30 miles for little or no pay, speaking to congregations that could not support a full-time pastor. It was exhausting work, but he knew God was up to something and had him moving just under the radar of the forces of evil. He walked righteously after Jesus, living as an example to his immediate family, as well as to his family in Suttontown.

It would seem the only thing the King family's farm lacked was tobacco. But Preacher Henry had made a covenant with God, who had delivered him from cigarettes many years prior.

In the midst of all this, the King family grew too. God blessed Preacher Henry and Donnie with nine children total, four daughters and five sons. First were Dorcas, Ruth, and Rachel—who was with the family only five months before she died a crib death. The next child was the first son, James Isaiah, and he was much loved by his father. He also died during the flu pandemic of 1918-1920, which claimed the lives of thousands of other North Carolinians. Preacher Henry mourned the loss of his firstborn son as long as he lived. But the family was soon blessed with another daughter, Esther, followed by four more sons: Samuel, Joseph, John, and the youngest, Moses, through whom the account of this family patriarch is preserved and presented.

Despite all the trials and heartache, God was certainly "up to something"! Could it be that this country preacher was setting in motion Kingdom principles still not well understood?

THE YOUNGEST SON IS BORN

America was still struggling with the stock market crash of the late 1920s when an 11-pound baby boy joined the Preacher Henry and Donnie King household. Moses Edmond was born on April 13, 1935, to a forty-year-old mother and a fifty-year-old father. With three sisters and three brothers to pamper him, this little guy was lavished with love. Little Moses was blessed with the very best source from which he learned values and life skills needed for the years ahead: a loving, godly family.

Times were difficult for many people during those days, but the King household was planted on the solid foundation of God's word. The family devotional pattern reveals a depth of Christian discipleship that remains a model for every Christian family.

They read the Bible together three times each day: at breakfast, dinner (lunch), and prior to bedtime. Preacher Henry read the Scriptures before breakfast and dinner. At supper, the family always said a table grace. Before bed each evening, Preacher Henry would gather the family together. Each member of the family had his or her own personal Bible and was expected to bring it to the evening devotions. The father began the devotional time by reading five verses of a particular Bible passage. Then Donnie King would read five verses, followed by each child from the oldest to the youngest. During this evening ritual, the family would read two or three chapters, depending on the length. The family used this method to read through the entire Bible and start again at Genesis 1:1. Following the Scripture readings, they all knelt by their chairs and in the same order as the readings, each one prayed aloud in his or her own manner.

There were heartaches and disappointments for the King family during these years, but God supplied every need. God even blessed the family with extra so they could share with neighbors in need, local churches, and the work of the North Carolina Conference. People could count on Preacher Henry to do some "heavy lifting" financially whenever a special need arose. But the good preacher never used these gifts to gain attention and honor for himself. He understood that he was simply an avenue of divine grace and this self-understanding in Christ enabled him to be used effectively for the Lord.

As Moses remembers these years in his own words, we had a wonderful African-American family move to our community in 1935. Uncle Rufus and Aunt Francis Peacock had four daughters: Lena, Mammie, Ophelia and Vinetta. They had one granddaughter, Lena Ruth, and later two grandsons, Clayton and Donald. They lived in one of our extra houses to help us work the land. They had been mistreated by their previous community in Johnston County, so they bonded quickly to the kindly Preacher Henry family and moved to the more tranquil community in Sampson County. God placed us together to fulfill His purposes. Members of this family continue to live as neighbors to the Kings.

It's a sad commentary on our area, but in those days the Ku Klux Klan was very active in Johnston County.[4] Many families were intimidated and sometimes were actually physically abused. Thus, the Peacock family made their "exodus" to a land with greater promise. With the Peacock family helping with the work, along with a tractor and other larger equipment

---

4. Since its early years, the Pentecostal Holiness Church has considered membership with the Ku Klux Klan, and other secret societies, as incompatible with membership in the church and contrary to the teachings of Jesus Christ.

to prepare the land, Preacher Henry was able to produce an abundance of commodities during a period when the demand was very high because of the second world war.

As with most family farms in our community, we had to work hard but we also had a lot to enjoy. The creek that ran behind our family farm provided the younger folks with a "swimming hole." Each spring we would clean away any debris, and many days in the hot summer we would eat a quick lunch and hurry to the swimming hole for a refreshing dip!

Many times when we had worked really hard or the weather was really hot, Daddy would bring us a special treat as a reward. Our favorite treats were pints of ice cream for each person or cinnamon buns. He would always bring these special treats when he was returning from the market in the late afternoon, when the day's work was done.

Like most successful men, Preacher Henry's success was greatly enhanced by his industrious wife Donnie. She would personally pack or supervise the packing of all the produce. It was very important that all packages in each lot be of the same size and quality. Buyers quickly figured out if a grower could be trusted to pack quality produce. While most growers would load and haul their produce to a shade tree to pack it for market, Donnie would work at the end of the rows in the sunshine because she could grade and pack more packages there.

Needless to say, everyone tried really hard to keep Mama happy! Before it was popular, she understood the concepts of "quality control"!

When teased about working in the sun, her answer was always the same, "The pickers have to pick in the sun, so I might as well pack in the sun." The family and workers knew that she was packing and watching everything from her vantage point at the end of the row. She could tell who was picking as they should and who was slack in their effort. She could also determine if a picker was pulling too much under-sized fruit. Needless to say, everyone tried really hard to keep Mama happy! Before it was popular, she understood the concepts of "quality control"!

On December 7, 1941, the United States of America was thrust into World War II. The six-year-old Moses King was just old enough to have a clear memory of the surprise attack on Pearl Harbor. During those years, local young men went to war and the King family eagerly listened to the news on the battery operated radio in the home's hallway. K. V. Kaltenborn and Gabriel Heatter were among Preacher Henry's favorite newscasters.[5]

---

5. K. V. Kaltenborn was a National Broadcasting Company (NBC) radio announcer during World War II. He was known for his excellent diction and in-depth analysis of events during the war. Gabriel Heatter was a radio broadcaster for the Mutual Broadcasting Network (MBN) during World War II. In the dark days of the war, especially in 1942, he was known for starting his broadcasts with the phrase, "Good evening everyone—There is good news tonight." His upbeat, optimistic accounts provided a great morale boost to the average American family listening nightly at home.

Moses' sister Ester's husband, Johnny, was drafted to serve in the war effort. An older brother, Samuel, was eighteen years old but was exempted to work on the farm. Preacher Henry's successful farming operation produced cotton, all kinds of food, meat, grain, and produce. Samuel was more valuable helping on the farm, as the family was part of a major effort to continue feeding the nation at war.

Many things were in short supply and had to be rationed, such as sugar, gasoline, and rice. The construction of electric lines was even halted because everything was being sent to the war effort. However, because the King farm produced so much food that was needed for the war, Preacher Henry was able to obtain a permit to buy a new John Deere Model B tractor in 1944. Until that time, the family had farmed everything with teams of mules or horses. While the tractor was a stripped-down model with steel wheels, had no starter, and was built to run on kerosene, it could do the necessary disking and land breaking far more efficiently than the mules and horses. In those days, having that kind of machinery was a big deal.

By the time the war was over, Preacher Henry had purchased his tobacco-growing family members' shares of the King land. Before long, with the introduction of more tractors and dependable people to help with the work, Preacher Henry was buying up most of the farmland that was offered for sale in the community. He had committed to never grow tobacco, so God trusted him to bring those acres into the fold of Christian dominion for the purposes of God's kingdom on earth.

Preacher Henry's faithfulness to God's standards proves again that God is up to something! He is moving upon his church to take dominion in this world! He has a divine strategy! God has a real purpose for every member of the body of Christ!

LIFE IN A CHANGING AMERICA

During the 1940s and 1950s, great change was under way in rural America and the King family alike. Many other local farmers began growing crops of produce to ship to the larger markets, just as Preacher Henry had been doing. A large number of produce buyers began to come to the area each year, and the Faison Fruit and Vegetable Exchange was opened. Here, buyers could bid on the day's offerings by the local growers. This created a new opportunity for growers to sell into the wholesale channels without having to ship directly to the Northern markets. Also, growers were paid in three days for their produce, which was guaranteed by the auction market.

It was during this time that Preacher Henry's work ethic instilled something in all our family that remains an inspiration to this day. The market opened at 9 a.m. and closed at 6 p.m., Monday through Saturday, and Preacher Henry sought to take three loads of produce each day. The family would rise early, pack the produce in bushel baskets, and load it for the early morning market. Preacher Henry would come back to the farm for lunch and take another load. Then he would leave around 5 p.m. to take a final load and finish the day. That was his plan, and everyone worked hard to make it happen. The buyers would yell across the sales yard, "Hey, Preacher, what are you harvesting tomorrow?" It was a great piece of Americana and rural eastern North Carolina history.

After the harvest of summer vegetables, which usually lasted until the first of August, Preacher Henry would load the family up and take them on a much needed vacation. The family would usually be away for about a week. Favorite vacation spots included the Great Smoky Mountains in North Carolina, the Blue Ridge Mountains of Virginia (and the caverns in those mountains), and visiting the nation's capital in Washington, D.C. While in Washington the family visited the great monuments, the Capitol, the White House, and especially the museums associated with the Smithsonian.

Other trips included visits to the North Carolina Atlantic coastline with ferry trips over to the Outer Banks. We always enjoyed one of the great stories of American history portrayed in the drama "The Lost Colony."[6] While on the Outer Banks, the family would visit Jockey's Ridge and Kill Devil Hills, and we would climb where the Wright brothers flew the first airplane.

The family cherished these respites from the hard labor on the farm. They would return to Sampson County ready to go back to work in late August in preparation for the fall harvest. In those years all cotton was hand-picked so we started picking as soon as the cotton started opening. Almost everyone helped with the cotton harvest. Our family and the Peacock family would average picking a 500-pound bale of ginned (deseeded) cotton each day. In the late afternoon we weighed each picker's day's harvest, and when completed, we would load enough cotton on Daddy's trailer to gin a large (500-pound) bale. These cotton bales were stored in a large barn and sold the next spring to pay the expense of farming the next year's crop. Stored cotton bales were like money in the bank!

But the harvest season did not end with cotton! The next harvest was sweet potatoes, which were sized and placed in bushel baskets to sell at the sweet potato auction. To ensure the best flavor, everyone worked hard to

---

6. "The Lost Colony" was first presented on July 4, 1937, on Roanoke Island. This was the 350th anniversary of the birth of Virginia Dare, the first English child born in North America.

harvest the sweet potatoes before the first killing frost. Sweet potatoes that were too small for market were sometimes sold to the cannery. They also made excellent livestock feed for the hogs and cattle.

People in America today do not understand how important it was to take care of your livestock in those years. The corn to feed the livestock was dry by the fall and ready to harvest. This harvest was the final harvest of the year. In earlier years the corn was harvested by hand and stored unshelled in large storage buildings called "cribs."

Before mechanical equipment, every farmer relied on horses or mules to help with the work. Corn and hay for these animals was very important. These animals were cared for and treated very well. In many instances these animals were like members of the family.

Sometimes, when the horses or mules had worked hard all day, people would walk to church for evening services rather than take the horse and buggy. This gave the animals time to rest and be ready for the next day of hard labor.

It was therefore necessary to store corn in a manner that ensured the livestock would have good feed until the next harvest. This was especially true for the horses and mules. In this part of North Carolina, the corn harvest usually lasted until Thanksgiving and the colder days of late autumn.

These cotton bales were stored in a large barn and sold the next spring to pay the expense of farming the next year's crop. Stored cotton bales were like money in the bank!

"Hog-killing" time in the South was also very important. Even today people use the phrase when it's cold, "It's cold enough to kill hogs." In those days on farms in eastern North Carolina this was an important time. This was true for the very prudent Preacher Henry household also.

Preacher Henry liked to have his "hog killing" between Thanksgiving and Christmas so the family could enjoy a fresh corned ham for the Christmas holidays. This holiday, celebrating the birth of our Savior Jesus Christ, was a very important event in those days on the farm. Slaughtering enough pork for a large family for an entire year took a lot of preplanning and a lot of people when the work was ready to be done. Usually two or three families would "trade help" on the killing days in order to get all the work completed. It usually took two days for the process to be completed for each family.

A hog killing occurred during a "cold spell." The work was mostly done outside in the barnyard near the smokehouse (a building where meats were cured). At the right time, neighbors came bundled up with a lot of warm clothing and arrived at the "crack of dawn." There were always two large fires: one fire heated the scalding vat, and the other fire heated hot water pots.

A designated person was in charge of keeping the water in the vat at the right temperature so that the hair of the slaughtered hog could be more easily removed. There was also a "fireman" who was responsible for the hot water for other sanitation needs while preparing the freshly cut meat into hams, shoulders, and streaks of lean bacon, sometimes called "side-meat." The larger cuts were "salted down" and placed in the smokehouse to begin the meat curing process. Properly cured meat would last all year without spoiling.

One of the well-loved features of a Southern hog killing was a big feast around midday. Everyone had started the work early and the weather was always cold, so this hot meal was an important part of the event. Two ladies were usually designated as the cooks for the meal and they always prepared a feast. In many ways, hog-killing time was as much a social event as a required food preservative event.

After the wonderful feast, most of the ladies began the process of preparing the "trimmings" into the lean and fat portions. The men continued to prepare the larger pieces of meat for the smokehouse. The lean trimmings were used to make the famous "hog-killing" country sausage that continues to set the standard for all pork sausage even today. The fat trimmings were placed in the large wash pots and cooked to make lard for the family's cooking needs.

The men were always interested in how many "stands" of lard the hog killing yielded. A stand usually weighed fifty pounds! They also measured the weight of the largest hams. Bragging rights belonged to the local farmer that had the largest hams and most "stands" of lard for that year! Preacher Henry, who had a reputation for his large and fine hogs, was always a strong contender in these local contests.

As the hog killing days closed and Christmas and another year followed, the King family was keenly aware of how God had manifested His grace and favor to them. As I grew older, I began to discern that the Holy Spirit was revealing principles related to the Kingdom of God and abundant living. Through my godly family, I began to realize that the Holy Spirit was up to something bigger than a successful farm.

A MOTHER'S GIFT OF LOVE FOR MISSIONS

Preacher Henry and his lovely wife Donnie Jennette had always put first their ministry and commitment to obey God's call in their lives. They did not try to "show off" their blessings; rather, they chose to live a modest lifestyle that reflected good judgment and good taste. In the day-to-day life of farming, they lived and passed along to their children the words of Jesus in Matthew 6:33, "Seek first the kingdom of God and His righteousness, and all these things shall be added to you."

Because of their single purpose of glorifying God through their work and ministry, the Holy Spirit would give them opportunities to channel His blessings to others. One such incident occurred when IPHC missionary Johnny Brooks and his wife, Erma Mae, visited the home.[7]

After Brother and Sister Brooks retired in the late 1940s from their missionary work in South Africa, they were assigned in 1952 to pastor the Saint Matthews and Goshen Pentecostal Holiness congregations. Early in 1954, while Rev. Brooks was the pastor at Goshen Church, God put it in his heart to return to Africa, specifically Nigeria, to pioneer the IPHC work there and build a Bible school.[8]

During the years the Brooks pastored the Goshen church, there were many opportunities for them to visit with the King family. Rev. Brooks knew that Preacher Henry had been the first Pentecostal Holiness missionary to Africa some forty years earlier. He and Preacher Henry had been friends since their days together at G. F. Taylor's Falcon Holiness School. By 1952, Preacher Henry had retired from pastoring, but still preached occasionally for local congregations and taught the adult Bible class at the Goshen Sunday School.

In 1954, as the word spread of Rev. Brooks returning to Africa, he visited the Preacher Henry home. While sitting around the dining room table and enjoying good fellowship, Donnie King asked Brother Brooks, "Are you really going to Nigeria?"

Brooks replied, "Yes."

Mrs. King, reflecting on the unfulfilled dreams of Henry and her nearly forty years earlier, said, "I've always wanted to be a missionary to West Africa, but I never had the opportunity."

Rev. Brooks wrote that she looked sad and intense as she spoke, "I have some money, $960 that I received as an inheritance from my father – it is all my inheritance – would you take it and do something in a permanent way – like helping to build a church – in Nigeria for me?"

Having listened to the conversation, Preacher Henry suggested that they add $40 of their own funds, to which Donnie gladly agreed. That night, they gave Brother Brooks $1,000 to build a church in a village called Nkek, Nigeria, which is close to the region in West Africa where Daddy had labored years ago.

---

7. Details of the Brooks' missionary life are in *The Simultaneous Principle: The History of IPHC World Missions the First 100 Years* by Frank G. Tunstall (Franklin Springs, GA: LifeSprings Resources, 2005).

8. Details of the following narrative are taken from *Mighty Moments: God's Leading Through a Life of Faith* by John W. Brooks (Franklin Springs, GA: Advocate Press, 1987) pp. 139-142, 182-184.

Rev. Brooks took the $1,000 and in 1955 placed it in a savings account, awaiting the right opportunity to use it. He used it to challenge the new-born Nigerian Pentecostal Holiness congregations to complete their buildings: "I want to give the money to the first congregation to finish their building. I'm not going to put Mrs. King's money in the ground, nor in the walls, but I will put it in the roof."

Several local congregations in West Africa worked diligently to complete their buildings, including one in Ghana. But the first one to complete their assignment was in the village of Nkek (pronounced Ng-kek). Rev. Brooks remarked, "It occurred to me that this was a very special coincidence; for Nkek is located right along the coast south of that strip in Liberia where Brother King had ministered years ago. I smiled as I imagined Mrs. King's delight at hearing the results of her gift."

That seed was planted and multiplied many times as other North Carolina churches heard about it and started giving to construct buildings in honor and memory of someone dear. Nkek Pentecostal Holiness Church, the "Donnie King Memorial Church", stands today, more than 50 years later, with King's picture gracing the vestibule as the congregation ministers the gospel of Jesus Christ. In today's currency, Donnie King's $960 would be worth approximately $10,000.[9] In the 1950s this was a large sum of money that the family, moved by the Holy Spirit, invested into God's kingdom. For me, the questions stirring in my heart were: What is the significance of this seed? What is God up to?

THE CHANGING OF THE GUARD

Preacher Henry and his beloved Donnie settled into their retirement years as the 1950s rolled on. Well into his 60s, the elder King continued to preach, advise his children, and lead a godly life. In the last year of his life, Preacher Henry's health progressively declined. On August 21, 1963, he entered into the presence of the Lord whom he had served for 78 years. Twenty-two months later, on June 30, 1965, Donnie King died of heart failure, and she left this world to be with Christ and join her husband before the Throne.

One can only wonder in amazement at the bond of these two soul mates as they served God faithfully, although ridiculed and scoffed at by their own families. While their bodies are no longer here on this earth, they left their DNA and their spiritual imprint on the many generations that followed.

God is up to something!

---

9. www.measuringworth.com.

Rev. Henry C. King – "Preacher Henry"

Donnie J. King

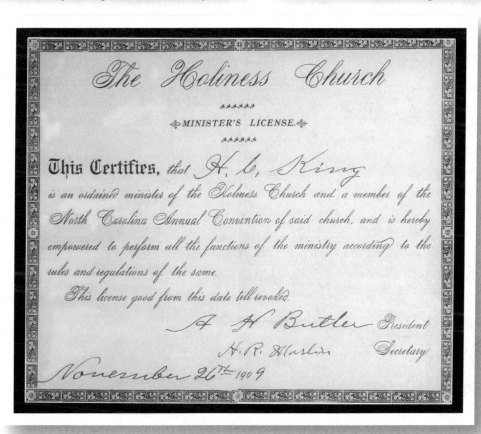

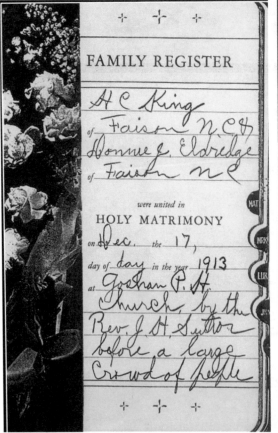

FAMILY REGISTER

A C King of Faison N.C. & Donnie J. Eldredge of Faison N C

were united in

HOLY MATRIMONY

on Dec. the 17, day of day in the year 1913 at Goshen P.H. Church, by the Rev. J. H. Sutton before a large Crowd of people

Henry C. King
and
Donnie J. Eldridge
on their wedding day.

December 17, 1913
Goshen P.H. Church

Farmers waiting to sell their produce at Mount Olive auction market during 1940s.

Farmers waiting at the cotton bin to have their seeded cotton ginned and baled. The cotton in each "sheet" of cotton on these trucks is one person's day's work picking cotton. This is an early 1940s photo.

Farmers at the Faison fruit and vegetable auction selling their produce in the mid 1950s.

Farmers with their ginned cotton at the cotton market in Mount Olive in the early 1920s. Each bale weighs around 500 lbs.

This log tobacco barn still stands today on the Ivey Farm in Wayne County. His type of curing barn was used in eastern North Carolina from 1900 to 1965.

Above: Preacher Henry and Donnie on vacation in the 1950s.

Left: Moses and his mother in front of the King home in the 1940s.

Right: Preacher Henry and Donnie with their grandchildren, Debbie and Gregg, in the early 1960s.

ding fellowship with any person engaged in those things referred to in Artice X of our government.

Thunder Swamp Church was reported by Slater Georgia Andrews, the delegate, and Bro. F. A. Dall also spoke of conditions there.

Upon motion, it was ordered that Rev. A. G. Canada visit Thunder Swamp Church and hold a meeting and explain the new discipline and take a vote of the church upon the matter of accepting the same.

An offering was taken upon the indebtedness of Kinston Tabernacle and there was given in cash and pledges One hundred, forty

Bro. H. C. King, having felt called of God as a missionary to Africa, was requested to speak concerning his call and the leadings of the Spirit in that direction.

After Brother King's statement, the Holy Ghost set His seal of approval upon it in a miraculous way through the interpretation of tongues, giving messages of encouragement and comfort, which were unmistakable in their assurances.

By motion, Bro. King was acknowledged as a worthy missionary and the Convention pledged him its support.

A collection was taken for missions and there was contributed $16.55.

amounting to $23.71.

Motion having passed, the Convention adjourned to meet again at 2:00 o'clock.

Benediction by Rev. A. H. Butler.

THIRD DAY—AFTERNOON SESSION.

Convention opened by singing "On the Sunny side", followed by prayer by Rev. C. B. Strickland.

A motion was made and passed ordering that the missionary offering of the morning session be given to Bro. H. C. King.

By motion, J. A. Culbreth was requested to speak in the interest of "The Apostolic Evangel," after which Revs. R. B. Jackson and A. H. Butler also made talks encouraging a wider circulation of the paper.

The committee on Ordination expressed their readiness to report, and Bro. G. F. Taylor of that committee made explanation concerning the application of Bro. N. B. Strickland, and after some

PROCEEDINGS

OF THE

Eleventh Annual Convention

OF

The Pentecostal Holiness Church

OF

North Carolina.

NOVEMBER 22, 23, 24, 1910.

GOLDSBORO, N. C.
NASH BROS., PRINTERS AND BINDERS,
1911.

FROM THE ORIGINALS
IN THE LIBRARY OF
Rev. W. Eddie Morris
Falcon, NC 28342

Preacher Henry's license and the 1910 minutes with motion to send him to the mission field in Africa.

The Henry and Donnie King Memorial Church in Nigeria that mother gave her $1,000 inheritance to help complete.

Moses poses in a field of sunflowers with the Preacher Henry home in the background.

This is an old livestock barn built in the mid 1940s by Preacher Henry to house mules and cattle.

SECTION
2

A New Generation

Moses and Dean King

SECTION 2

A New Generation

I learned so much from my parents, siblings, and church people that it is impossible to talk about my life without an understanding and appreciation of them. Most of the story that follows cannot be separated from the rich blessings and training I received from my parents.

But my story also includes God's wonderful provision for me of a godly wife! Geraldine Best was my high school sweetheart. I knew that she was "the one" meant for me and I loved her deeply.

On July 23, 1955, a few months after I turned twenty years old, Geraldine, who was eighteen, and I were married in a double wedding with our best friends, Jesse Lindsay and Hilda Coley. Rev. Ralph Jernigan, a minister in the North Carolina Conference of the Pentecostal Holiness Church, performed the ceremony. My new bride and I lived with the Preacher Henry household for about a year until a house could be prepared for us.

My father, Preacher Henry, always allowed his sons to farm 1.5 acres of farmland beginning at age sixteen. We planted whatever we chose and used the proceeds to start a nest egg. I always planted my acreage in bell peppers because they usually did well on the market. After three years, I built a laying house with my funds and began raising pullets (young hens) for laying eggs to sell on the open market.

Geraldine (whom I had lovingly nicknamed "Dean") was an incredibly smart and industrious lady. In my eyes, she looked like a baby doll, but her beauty did not keep her from being an industrious and diligent wife and mother. Soon after we were married, we were able to cash flow enough funds to expand into hog production. This was due not only to our own efforts, but also thanks to my father, who always gave his children a sow (mother hog) with piglets as a wedding gift. With this lovely, industrious lady by my side, I was inspired to think big thoughts and dream big dreams.

On May 31, 1957, our first child was born. We named the handsome 8-pound, 8-ounce boy Moses Gregg and called him "Gregg."

As our family grew, the farm business was also expanding. We had a contract for producing fertile eggs with Clinton Hatchery. We sold furrow-to-finish slaughter hogs to Lundy Packing Company. We employed Ophelia Peacock Smith and her son, Clayton, to help with the day-to-day chores of poultry and livestock. I learned great lessons leading them and managing the field crops.

On October 20, 1960, we welcomed our second child, a small but beautiful little girl. We named her Deborah Dean and called her "Debbie." She was born small and required extra care for a few weeks, but she was a doll baby, just like her mom.

Things were going well with the farming. God blessed the long hours and hard work. Though we worked five and six days a week, we nonetheless remembered our spiritual roots and were in church on Sunday and other times during the week. Family life was busy as we spent time with my aging father. The home was active with our young son Gregg, while Debbie was 18 months old and walking all over the place.

It was then that someone noticed Debbie had begun bumping into a support column in the middle of the living area where Daddy was convalescing. Further investigation revealed that Debbie was losing her sight for no apparent reason. She was referred to Duke Hospital, where she was eventually diagnosed with a degenerative disease of the central nervous system. There was little the doctors could do for her. Her prognosis was a slow death, and Dean and I were devastated as we watched our baby girl lose her battle for life. Taking care of her was a full-time job at our home. Four years after being diagnosed, our precious little girl went home to be with the Lord on September 21, 1966.

The middle 1960s were a difficult time for us. We entered a grieving season as we buried my father, my mother, and Debbie in a three-year period. We did not understand how this could be. But in spite of our questions and sorrow, we chose to trust in God!

MEANWHILE, BACK ON THE FARM

Though our hearts were broken during these years, the farm continued to do well. Like Jacob in the Bible (Genesis 30:30), our flocks and herds were increasing. An added blessing was that by 1963 we had earned and saved enough assets to join our friend, Jesse Lindsay, and his brother, Elmon, in opening our first Piggly Wiggly grocery store in Clinton, North Carolina. Our family was able to provide funding while the Lindsay brothers managed the day-to-day business responsibilities. We were three equal partners.

How could this be? I was only twenty-eight years old and Dean was only twenty-six, and yet God had channeled through us most of the funds to start this new Piggly Wiggly store. What was God up to?

A NEW DAUGHTER

After Debbie was laid to rest, there was a hollowness that begged to be filled, and God blessed our home with another darling little girl. Janet Carol was born on December 19, 1967, just in time for Christmas. She brought much joy to the King home. Gregg had suffered almost silently as Debbie had slowly drifted from us, but now there was another sister for Gregg and all of us to love.

Janet was a beautiful, blue-eyed, blonde little girl. Everyone admired her! Gregg was our handsome, ten-year-old son with great presence and poise. Dean and I felt that our family was complete and life was good. We had built a new home in 1965, and we were finally able to look ahead, away from the pain and grief of losing our Debbie.

We worked hard on the farm and God continued to bless our efforts. The Piggly Wiggly store was also doing well and producing nice profits. Life was good down on the farm! However, unbeknownst to us, there was a dark cloud forming just over the horizon.

TRAGEDY STRIKES AGAIN

In the early days of 1974, we became aware that our dear Janet was beginning to lose focus in school. She had done well in kindergarten and until mid-year of the first grade, but some issues were causing concern. We were told that at best, she would grow out if it, and at worst, it would be a manageable issue.

As I returned home one night after doing some visitation work in the community for the church, Dean met me at the door in tears. I immediately asked, "What's the problem?" Dean replied that Janet had gone to bed early and was soon discovered by her mother in a violent, convulsive condition. We had experienced convulsions with our little Debbie, our deceased daughter, so terrible fear gripped our hearts. I immediately called Janet's doctor at the clinic, and we lovingly cradled her in our arms and transported her to the doctor's office for assistance.

After briefly observing Janet's condition, the nurse called for urgent transport to Duke Hospital. With tears in her eyes, Dean rode in the ambulance with Janet, and I returned home to quickly get the things needed for a hospital stay. As I drove back into the garage upon returning home, I found myself crying out to God in an audible voice and begging Him not to take us through this type of tragedy again. However, she was placed in the trauma unit, where her convulsive activity continued until the next evening.

This is unthinkable. How can this be? How will we bear this long, painful ordeal again? Please, Lord—Please, help me!

There were many questions begging to be answered, but there were very few answers. The days, weeks, months, and years ahead would be painful ones as this beautiful, blue-eyed six-year-old faced odds not easily described. Gregg, who was seventeen years old, handsome, and intelligent (140-plus IQ), struggled with what was going on with his little sister, as well as his parents' pain.

Please tell me, what is a brother to do? What is a mother to do? The pain of death is one thing, but how would Dean deal with birthdays and Christmases and—the list just goes on and on. What is a mother to do as the years creep by and her friends' little girls grow up and bring joy to their lives and laugh and play and—what is this mother to do? Dads, well now, everyone knows that dads are strong, but dads have breaking hearts too. Dads must be strong for the family. They *must* be strong— they must be strong because they are dads, but what's a dad to do when there are no answers?

There were seven years of questions and struggles before God called this precious little girl home at the age of thirteen. The smile on her face at passing was confirmation that God is still on His throne, and those who trust Him will often trust Him without their questions being answered in their earthly lives.

We learned many things in those years, including that for some things there are not answers this side of heaven. But we also learned that "God is able to make all grace abound toward you; that ye, always having all sufficiency in all things, may abound to every good work" (2 Corinthians 9:8).

There were many questions begging to be answered, but there were very few answers. The days, weeks, months, and years ahead would be painful ones as this beautiful, blue-eyed six-year-old faced odds not easily described.

CHANGE IS IN THE AIR

As we moved toward the 1970s, there were forces at work behind the scenes that were drastically changing agriculture in the United States. Large corporations entered food production and started reshaping the food supply chain. Vertical integration was beginning in poultry; it even moved into pork production but at a slower pace. *Vertical integration* meant that the whole process of food production to the market was under common ownership and control. In practice this market mechanism made it difficult for smaller farmers and producers to survive.

We were semi-vertically integrated and knew we would lose our markets at some point. Prudent planning was needed to avoid financial injury. Therefore, we began drawing down our farming operation in poultry and livestock in the early 1970s and started looking for investment opportunities off the farm in order to secure our future.

We had acquired a choice property in the small town of Mount Olive, North Carolina. We invested in and developed the property, building and operating another Piggly Wiggly there. This proved to be a prudent strategy, which allowed us to spin off our interest later with the Lindsay brothers into our new corporation and run our own retail super-marketing company .

The late 1970s and the 1980s were years of great change and challenge. There was much lost opportunity because of misplaced leadership and misused resources in our retail partnership with the Lindsay brothers. But God is still God, and He is faithful to fulfill His word: "And God is able to make all grace abound toward you; that ye, always having all sufficiency in all things, may abound to every good work" (2 Corinthians 9:8).

BRICK AND MORTAR FUNDS

God set a plan in motion in the late 1970s, as the Holy Spirit began prompting me to invest personal funds into various ministries that had building projects underway. As a young teenager, a seed had been put in my heart as I had witnessed my mother plant her $960 inheritance in a church in Nigeria through Rev. Johnny Brooks.

I consulted my attorney about creating a foundation for such purposes, and he correctly suggested that the best plan to accomplish this type of giving was through an established church stewardship department. In this way, I would not be burdened with all the annual IRS filings and the many compliance issues that come along with IRS regulations.

For this level of giving, I determined that I would donate $1,000 to any church building project that requested a donation, stipulating that it would be invested in their church facility and not used for church operating expenses. I was planting a financial seed into buildings that would proclaim the gospel of Jesus Christ long after I was deceased. I lovingly called this my "Brick and Mortar Ministry" because of the connotation of permanence associated with such building materials.

As I reflect on the many years of this ministry and the fruit that has come forth, I find myself asking, "What are God's purposes for us? What is God up to?"

A NEW BUSINESS MODEL

In the early 1990s, it was becoming increasingly obvious that our existing business model was flawed. It was determined that since all three partners each had a grown son, we were approaching the time for a new business model. This would prove to be quite a challenging endeavor, especially for me. I was in business with my best friend and his brother. The need to separate our varied assets in a way that served each one's needs was difficult, to say the least.

THE UNTOLD STORY

Relationships have always had great value to me. How could I negotiate these difficult issues and maintain a proper relationship with my friends? I prayed for guidance, and based on that guidance assembled a plan. After discussing the facts with my attorney, a correct plan was put into motion. I instructed my attorney to select an outside accountant that would handle all the numbers for the separation of assets. I placed both the attorney and the accountant on continuing retainer to represent my interests with our company accountant and partners. I informed all parties by certified mail, and our plan was put in motion.

My role in the separation was only to advise and consent. My attorney and accountant were from outside of our market area, which permitted them to be uninhibited and to negotiate wisely. After more than a year, we still had many unresolved issues.

But a life-changing event occurred one very average August summer morning in 1992. The Holy Spirit spoke to me "in my spirit and in my ears" these words from Proverbs 3:5, 6: "Lean not to your own understanding, but trust also in Me, and I will direct thy path."

I leaped from my bed and took pen and paper, and I wrote those words down for record. I wept before the Lord. As I pondered those words of the Holy

Spirit, I was immediately drawn to the words of Jesus, when He was asked about the greatest commandment: "Master, which is the great commandment in the law? Jesus said unto him, *'Thou shalt love the Lord thy God with all thy heart, and with all thy soul, and with all thy mind. This is the first and great commandment. And the second is like unto it, Thou shalt love thy neighbor as thyself. On these two commandments hang all the law and the prophets'"* (Matthew 22:36-40, emphasis added).

The Holy Spirit spoke to me "in my spirit and in my ears" these words from Proverbs 3:5, 6: "Lean not to your own understanding, but trust also in Me, and I will direct thy path."

As I considered the words of Jesus, it became painfully clear to me. Jesus said that he had come to fulfill the law. As a Christian, I was in Him and, therefore, He was prompting me to love my neighbors (or business partners) as much as I loved my own personal interests and desires.

My life was forever changed as I struggled with those words of Jesus. To be led by the Holy Spirit, I had to start being very careful to measure my decisions in every human endeavor by Jesus' own words. I began to understand how the divine laws of heaven should take precedence over the natural laws of our "human experience." I began to comprehend more fully what it meant to take up our cross and follow Jesus.

MAJOR ISSUES ARE RESOLVED

In the context of this new revelation knowledge, we began making proposals that were unjustified in the natural, but which fit more closely with the words of Jesus. We were able to complete the work by December of that year, and on December 26, 1992, a new operating model was put into action. We led a portion of the same employees with new dynamics and new purpose, and we focused on the words spoken by the Holy Spirit into my life experience on that ordinary August morning. Because we were obedient to His commands, God led us into a level of accomplishment that we could not have even imagined.

THE BUILDING THE HOLY SPIRIT LEASED

This incident, which occurred in the period 1991-92, I am sharing with guarded reservations. *It is a God thing!* It is so precious that it should be respected and revered as a testimony to the active involvement of the Holy Spirit in the personal life of the believer.

In 1988, Wal-Mart was rolling toward North Carolina, opening stores all across the Southeast. We had an anchor tenant in our property, The Maxway Company from Sanford, North Carolina. Their Mack's stores were an outstanding middle-market retailer that was into soft goods and all types of other domestic goods, just above the Dollar Stores' operating format. The Maxway stores had a fifteen-year lease with two five-year options. When their lease term was completed in 1988, the company notified our office that they would be closing operations in our property because of the reshaping of the retail landscape.

The property was larger than was needed for many other retailers, so I began looking at how to best divide the building for two or three tenants. Meanwhile, The White Stores of Greenville, which was another quality middle-market retailer, suffered a roof collapse in a portion of their building, so they requested to move their merchandise into our building for liquidation. We were hopeful that they would use our location and a permanent lease would result, but they, like Mack's stores, had decided to exit the market because of the effect that Wal-Mart's expansion was having on middle-market retailers.

After exhaustive efforts to redesign the space and lease it to other prospective tenants, it seemed that all efforts led to a dead end of disappointing results. I often went to the property and sat or walked around, praying for guidance about how to move forward, but nothing seemed to happen.

TALKING TO THE PROPERTY

There are a few things that will always make us a little bit suspect of losing our sanity. One such thing is when we start talking to ourselves. Another is when we start talking to *things*. Still another is when we get so bold as to start speaking out loud to the Lord and asking the Holy Spirit to do something in the physical arena.

On this ordinary spring morning in 1991, after exhausting my best efforts at leasing the property, I drove into the parking lot and parked in front of the vacant building. As I stepped outside the car and looked toward the building, a spirit of excitement rose up within me. It was as if I were engaging the Holy Spirit as another person, on a more personal level than I had ever experienced. I found myself standing outside my car and talking just as if I were talking to a person—but I spoke to that building.

I said to the building, "You are not serving the purposes you are supposed to serve. You are not producing any revenue. I command you in Jesus' name to fulfill your purpose and produce revenue."

I spoke to the Holy Spirit as if I were talking to a realtor. I said, "I have done all I know to do. I have contacted all my contacts, and I really have just failed in my efforts." I continued, "Lord, you know stuff I don't know, and I believe there is someone that needs this building. They may be in town or out of town; I don't know. They may not even know now that they need this building, but You know. I am asking You to take charge of this property as if it were Yours, for it is Yours."

I continued speaking to the Holy Spirit in this manner, "This is what I have been asking for the property. I would also appreciate any increases or additional perks that You might be able to get. Now I'm placing this in Your hands, and I thank You, that You are an ever-present help in our time of need. Now, I thank You for Your favor."

I was not on a spiritual high. I did not feel any special emotional high, just the deep, settled peace of God that attends our every day as Christians. I closed my car door and walked to my office, like any other day, and I quickly put this experience in a treasured place in my mind and forgot about it for a while.

THE TELEPHONE CALL

Some months later, I was taking a much-treasured Sunday afternoon nap on the couch. The telephone rang, and Dean answered it as usual.

"It's for you, Moses," she said.

"Who is it?" I asked.

"It's a Mr. Gordon. He is with the U.S. Postal Service in Greensboro," she replied.

"I wonder why in the world he would be calling me on a Sunday afternoon," I replied. "Okay, I'll get it."

"Hello, Mr. King," he began. "You own property in Mount Olive that would meet a need the Postal Service has, and I would like to schedule an appointment with you, if possible, for tomorrow to discuss using your building as a temporary location for the post office."

The words *temporary location* rang negatively in my ear, and I expressed my concern with him based on my most recent experience with The White Stores. Businesses moving into a location and then moving out soon after can sometimes stigmatize property with a negative connotation when it comes to prospective tenants. (Frequent turnover can give the appearance that businesses are not succeeding due to the location.)

"Yes, I do understand your concern," he replied, "but I would really like to discuss this further, as I have a very urgent need to vacate our present location, so that a crew can remove some asbestos from the building. I would like to use your building for six months."

"Okay," I replied. "I'll be glad to meet with you, but Mondays are very busy for me. How about later in the week?"

"I plan to be in Mount Olive tomorrow relative to our problem," he responded. "Maybe we could meet later in the day?"

"Okay, if you will be in town anyway, let's meet at 4 p.m. at my office," I replied.

As I moved back to my treasured position on the couch, I was commenting to my wife, Dean, that his proposition had a lot of negatives. Mr. Gordon really just needed a favor (grace), just like The White Stores had needed a favor (grace) a year earlier. As I took a comfortable position to complete my Sunday afternoon relaxation, I was reminded of the words spoken by Jesus when asked what the greatest command of all was. His words rang crystal clear to me as He added that the second-most important commandment was to love your neighbor as yourself.

Could it be that God was revealing new insight to me regarding kingdom principles and kingdom living? Could it be that Mr. Gordon's need was, in fact, my neighbor in need? What was God up to? What should I do?

THE MONDAY MEETING

Mr. Gordon showed up for our meeting promptly on Monday afternoon. We had dispensed with staff meetings and advertising, along with the other weekly functions that are an important part of a typical Monday at our office, so everything was right on schedule.

After considering Mr. Gordon's request to use the building temporarily and asking God for wisdom earlier during my personal devotion, I was impressed to propose a single payment of $25,000 for the use of the building for six months. When I suggested to Mr. Gordon what I felt was a proper approach to resolving his problem and meeting the need of the Postal Service, he smiled with amazement.

He responded, "That is exactly what I had in mind because that's my limit of authority for spending for such matters. Otherwise, I will have to go through much red tape requesting funding, and that can take several months. With this proposal, I can move quickly."

"Would you like to see the building?" I asked.

"No, that's not necessary. My real estate department has already acquired adequate information from the public domain at the county courthouse," Mr.

Gordon answered. "We will need your approval to build some interior walls and make some improvement on the rear dock area for our trucks. Of course, this will not cost you anything, and we will leave the improvements in place or we will remove them when we leave the premises—whichever you prefer. I so much appreciate your helpfulness. I know we can work together, and you have my word that you will be pleased with our use of the property and the improvements that we make."

With that, Mr. Gordon suggested that he would personally hand-deliver the agreement for my signature, along with payment, to our office in two days, and he left for his drive back to Greensboro. When the payment was received and the agreement was signed, I still believed that this was only about doing the right thing. It was important to me that I helped my neighbor in need; but was there another purpose coming into focus?

THE POST OFFICE RELOCATES

After the construction crew had made their improvements and all the lockboxes were moved and made ready to serve the public, we were amazed at the activity and traffic that the post office brought to the shopping area and to our Piggly Wiggly store, which was located there. Many customers commented about how convenient it was to have the post office there.

We were all quite pleased, but the political operatives and "old money" families in town were very envious. How did the Kings, who were from the country, fall into such a favored position with the Postal Service? The explanation many settled on was, "They must have some powerful connections in Washington." It seemed that the city policy makers and the local political operatives had not been consulted, and this caused quite a stir with the "talking heads" around town.

Even so, things went well with the post office at their new location. The local postmaster became a close business friend, and he quickly established himself as an advocate for all things that favored my best interests. After about five months, he called me to the side as I was leaving the post office lobby.

"Do you have a minute to talk?" he asked.

"Why, yes, I guess so," I replied.

As we stepped into his office, he closed both doors for privacy. "Would you be interested in talking to Mr. Gordon about a permanent lease on this property?" he asked.

"I thought you were going to remove the asbestos from the old post office building and refurbish it," I responded.

"That building will not be adequate for our future growth, and the cost to remodel it is coming in extremely high," he replied. "I like this building and the location is ideal. I don't get to decide on these matters, but I can affect the outcome."

He continued, "With your permission, I will make the suggestion that we ask for another twelve-month temporary lease extension. If we relocate or stay here, we have a legal obligation to let the public have input into the decision. It will take twelve months to advertise in the newspaper and let all interested persons bid to provide a new permanent post office building. According to the law, we have to go through this process, and then a study of each location must be completed."

With that information, I responded that the "old money" families and the local political operatives in town would likely have the advantage. They would likely build and lease a new post office building to the Postal Service.

"You have an existing building in the right location in town, and it is expandable for future growth, if needed," he responded. "We are already located here, and as postmaster, I like the facility," he reassured me.

With this, the discussion ended. As I left the lobby of the post office and looked across the parking lot, I suddenly remembered that warm, sunny spring morning almost a year earlier when I asked God to help me lease that building and released it into his hands. I remembered my own words in prayer to God: "Lord, somebody needs this building, but I can't find them. They may be right here in town. I just don't know, but somebody needs this building. I ask You for Your help and I thank You for Your help in Jesus' name. Now I praise You for Your favor and goodness to me."

As I returned to my office, I was in awe at the magnitude of what was going on in my life. I knew, without a doubt, that I had encountered the hand of God intervening in the affairs of man. I felt that God was up to something exciting, and I needed to be very careful not to touch His glory or claim any credit for what was transpiring.

I purposed to treat these treasures of insight as very private and precious. I shared them with no one but my family. I followed the counsel of the Holy Spirit that had been revealed to me on that August morning a few months earlier: "Lean not to your own understanding, but trust also in Me, and I will direct thy path."

In that moment, I wondered how God would lead us through the onslaught of efforts by others to gain this prized lease. Though I had many questions and was unsure of the outcome, I decided to trust in God and follow his leadings.

NOTE: Let me offer a side note for the reader who is not familiar with these matters. A lease with the U.S. Postal Service is a one-of-a-kind asset. These leases are as valuable as money, and they are much sought after. They are bought and sold. Even today, our office receives inquiries almost weekly seeking to purchase our post office lease with or without the building.

A 30-YEAR LEASE IS SIGNED

Following my discussion with the postmaster, we granted another temporary twelve-month lease extension and soon received a proposed permanent lease prototype for our consideration. Meanwhile, the public was informed of the decision to relocate the post office permanently. The political operatives and "talking heads" all rushed in to try and win favor for their property and, of course, to establish any negatives they could in regard to our property.

One of the strongest politicians in town made multiple trips to Washington, talking with his connections there. Several interested property owners had Washington connections also, and several senators and congressmen came to our town to try and influence the decision of where the new post office would be located.

Meanwhile, I was moving just under the radar of the public view to allow God to be sovereign in this situation. I decided I would not use any of my political connections. I would not use the counsel of any lawyers, real estate brokers or other persons, who might want to claim credit for a successful negotiation. The Postal Service was taking lease proposals for a twenty-year lease. I felt it would be a prudent approach to quote them both a twenty-year lease and also a more advantageous lease (for both the leaser and the lessee) for thirty years.

This proved to be a good strategy, as the Postal Service quickly moved to accept the thirty-year proposal. As soon as the legal time limit for public input had elapsed, we had in our possession a signed thirty-year lease, which would impact our business interests in many positive ways. God, by his Holy Spirit, responded to a need that I had lifted up to Him by providing me with an invaluable lease, just like He had impressed on me to reach out to the need Mr. Gordon had brought to me for a six-month temporary lease for the Postal Service two years earlier.

What was God up to? To this day, the "talking heads" are still trying to figure out what kind of connection the King family has with the powers that be. They are confronted with this same pestering question every time they make their daily trip to the post office.

Could it be that when Jesus spoke His reply to the Pharisees about which was the greatest commandment of all, He was speaking to all generations a profound key to kingdom living? Have we been much quicker to embrace the first commandment, "Thou shalt love the Lord thy God with all thy Heart," than we have the second commandment, "Thou shalt love thy neighbor as thyself"? Can it be that God wants us to pick up this key to kingdom living and open the door of kingdom abundance into our human experience? Can it be that our self-centeredness has slammed that door shut while we stand and sing out loud, "Hallelujah, praise God from whom all blessings flow," yet still walk down a path of lack as Christians?

Is God's kingdom in this world only inside us, or does God's kingdom on this earth exist in the domain of our human experience, when we humbly "flesh out" or follow these two commandments as we walk among men?

When Jesus prayed in the model prayer (Matthew 6:9-13), "Thy kingdom come, Thy will be done in earth, as it is in heaven," what greater kingdom principles did he have in mind? "Thy kingdom come. Thy will be done in earth, as it is in heaven." Is God's kingdom in this world only inside us, or does God's kingdom on this earth exist in the domain of our human experience, when we humbly "flesh out" or follow these two commandments as we walk among men? What is God trying to reveal to us? "And God is able to make all grace [favor] abound toward you; that ye, always having all sufficiency in all things, may abound to every good work" (2 Corinthians 9:8).

A NEAR-DEATH EXPERIENCE

My son, Gregg, who was astute in business, and my wife, Dean, who is proficient and prudent in all things, joined me to complete my administrative team. It was challenging and exciting to work together, knowing that God was up to something and we were following His lead. We immediately began to see profits rebound, and we were enjoying working together in our new roles as administrators of a new and better operating model.

However, in late May of 1993, something was going terribly wrong with my health. I tried to ignore the symptoms, but finally called my primary care doctor and shared what I was experiencing. He advised me to come to his office immediately, and after examining me, he seemed puzzled. He remarked that he didn't know what was going on, but he was going to call Dean and inform her that he was admitting me to the hospital for testing, and I was not allowed to be driving.

I slumped to the floor beside the chair as my doctor left the room and began to weep and pray. *What, Lord, is going on? I am following Your lead and I need to be with my family and employees.*

I was soon admitted to the local hospital and continued a downward spiral into almost nothingness. The consulting surgeon and lab technician both suggested transferring me to the specialists at the University of North Carolina at Chapel Hill hospital; however, my primary care physician didn't agree. After three days of tests and no answers, Dean informed our doctor that she intended to move me on Monday, with or without his approval. She asked again for him to arrange a transfer. He reluctantly agreed, and a transfer was set for Monday at noon.

Meanwhile, I continued to drift downward on Saturday night and Sunday morning. But late on Sunday morning, I realized I was becoming stable and more responsive. What was going on? After I reflected on the timing, I realized that the body of Christ was together praying for me during church time, and God's healing grace had been extended to my need.

On Monday, I was transferred to the UNC hospital infectious disease unit for close evaluation. A team of three staff doctors was assigned to my case, and after about three hours they appeared together at my bedside and announced their conclusion. First, I was extremely anemic, and second, because of the weakened condition caused by the anemia, I had contracted Legionnaires' disease. They started treatment right away.

The head doctor remarked again in a reassuring tone, "You are going to require close supervision for seven days with intravenous medication, after which you must have complete bed rest for an additional fourteen days and ingest the medication orally. Our blood analysis shows that you decided to live about 24-28 hours ago."

At that, I shared how I had stopped my physical descent at church time on Sunday as the body of Christ lifted me up in prayer. He smiled and replied, "It's always good to pray."

The recovery was slow and painful. The doctors soon ordered a 24/7 intravenous treatment that would be powerful enough to control the Legionella bacteria. The side effects of this treatment were intense burning of the veins, with swelling that would close off the medication's gateway into the bloodstream. Therefore, the needle carrying the medication had to be moved to a new location every 6-12 hours. The treatments were painful. There was a lot of abusive searching for new veins on my arms and legs. Finally, the caregivers had to resort to deep muscle veins in order to complete the treatment.

When released from the hospital, I had several long weeks of house confinement, while Gregg and Dean carried the full weight of our business enterprises. Both are strong and capable leaders, but they were tested to the fullest extent because it was midsummer, and we were still carrying on the family tradition of wholesale vegetable production in addition to operating the Piggly Wiggly supermarkets.

To put into perspective the full magnitude of their load of responsibility, they had 125-plus people on payroll operating the supermarkets, and 40-50 people working in the harvesting and packing of vegetables every day. We were a large producer of eggplant, and our operating model was set to harvest and pack 1,000 bushel crates each day. We could literally supply the market with eggplant in the eastern U.S. markets, so managing the harvest was very important. The fields had to be irrigated properly and the harvested fruit had to be handled and cooled properly to satisfy our very discreet and quality sensitive customers. I had to watch the trucks come and go to the packinghouse as the four-week harvest progressed, without being able to assist my family.

Sometimes in our life experiences, the timing can seem terribly wrong. Why did I become ill right in the middle of harvest time? Also, our new retail company was only six months old, and strong leadership was needed in this very competitive marketplace. As the days passed by, I slowly regained my vigor and vitality. I also gained a more complete understanding of what it really means to trust God in all things. As I returned to a regular level of responsibility and work, I pondered many of these things in my heart and mind. What was God up to?

I was always reminded of the words spoken to me, just one short year earlier on that ordinary August morning: "Lean not to your own understanding, but trust also in me, and I will direct thy paths." Could it be that the Holy Spirit (our counselor) was teaching me that the "God factor" is more important than the "me factor"?

God is always up to something. His favor abounds to us! Again I learned the power of His Word, "And God is able to make all grace [favor] abound toward you; that ye, always having all sufficiency in all things, may abound to every good work (2 Corinthians 9:8).

A DECADE OF AMAZING CONQUESTS

"Lean not to your own understanding, but trust also in me, and I will direct thy path." Did I hear those words in my spirit, or were they spoken audibly on that August morning in 1992 as I lay in my bed? This is the question that always arises when we talk about hearing God speak to us. I will affirm to you that I heard those words with every fiber of my being. My spirit, my ears, my mind, my everything was awash with these words from the Lord.

We often lack the analytical ability to define exactly on which level we encounter God, since we are both spirit and flesh. The truth is it does not matter so much how God speaks to us. What matters most is that we get a word from God, recognize His voice, and are obedient to His commands. My life was forever changed as I learned to follow His gentle leadings in all things. I learned anew the importance of loving God supremely and loving others within my domain of influence (my neighbors) as myself. Not only was the supply of God's abundance released into our lives, but also, as the word of the Lord says, "He lifted up my head. He gave favor whenever favor was needed. He allowed us to serve Him on a higher level as we learned to follow His leadings."

We were honored in 1995 with the prestigious national Spirit of America Award, presented by the National Grocers Association. This award is given in recognition of excellence in business and humanitarian projects. In 1997, we were honored with the National Piggly Wiggly Operator of the Year Award for business and community service excellence. Also in 1997, we were elected to the National Piggly Wiggly Operators Association Board of Directors for a five-year tenure, which culminated in serving as national president and convening our national convention at the Grand Hyatt Hotel Convention Center in Washington, D.C., in 2001.

Why would God lift up his children in this world? Because God has a purpose for us. We are His witnesses and the product of His grace. What are His purposes? What is God up to?

A NEW ASSIGNMENT FROM GOD

On January 10, 2004, I received a prophetic word from the Lord. It was in four distinct directives, so I quickly took my pen, wrote these words down and tucked them in my Bible, where they remain until this day:

1. Look back and acknowledge that God has been with you in the past.
2. There will be miracles of directions.
3. I will give miracles of conquest over permanents.[1]
4. I will give miracles of provision with what you already have.

These prophetic words rang clear in my spirit as I penned them and pondered them in my mind. Then, I somewhat pushed them to the back of my

---

1. That is, things the world presumes to be permanent, unchangeable, can be changed by God.

mind. Meanwhile, as the months passed by and the autumn season set in, I received a phone call from my attorney.

"I will be closing my practice in a few months," he stated. "I would like for you to select another person to handle your legal affairs, so I can transfer your files to them," he continued.

"What is the reason for your decision?" I asked. "You are much younger than I am. Have you decided to retire?"

"My doctor has advised me that I have advanced cancer of the larynx," he replied, "and it will require very radical treatment with rest, and I have chosen to decline the treatment and focus on the rest. I want to enjoy a better quality of life than this type of treatment often allows. I will trust my health to God and nature."

After expressing my concerns and sorrow, I thanked him for his call and assured him I would be back in touch. With this information I was confronted with some new realities. My estate plan was in place, but it was very open ended. We had talked many times over the years about my passion for investing in church buildings. We had discussed my father and mother's roles in ministry and how my father had not just been a minister, but had also always been there financially when large projects needed his support. I had also enjoyed our "Brick and Mortar" ministry, but I always knew that I wanted to fund an endowment that would continue this ministry after I was deceased.

Now I knew I must pray for wisdom and insight. The Lord would be faithful to lead as I focused on putting His purposes first, while I studied and meditated on His word. Our God is a big God. As He began to illuminate my intellect and reveal His purposes, I got all excited. I said to God, "Wow, I like this plan! This is exciting. Why yes, we can do this!" What was God's plan and purpose for us? What was God up to?

Mount Olive Piggly Wiggly
This store features two sit-down dining rooms and a Southern cooking kitchen and bakery, a butcher shop meat department, a large fresh produce department, florist, garden center, pharmacy and financial services department, along with the standard supermarket merchandise.

The Mount Olive Post Office as it is today, located next to Piggly Wiggly.

Moses addressing the national convention in Washington D.C. in 2001 as national president.

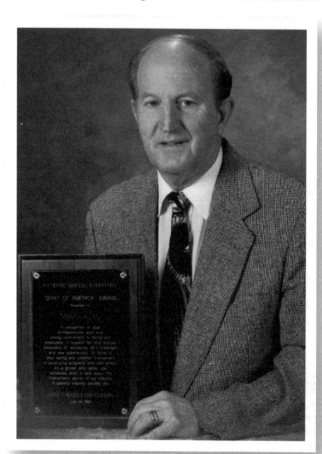

Moses receives the Spirit of America Award in 1995 from the National Grocers Association.

Above: Moses is presented with the National Owner/Operator of the Year award in 1997 at the Opryland Hotel and Convention Center in Nashville, Tennessee.

Moses and Dean celebrate their 50th wedding anniversary with their family and friends in the Great Smoky Mountains of North Carolina.

It doesn't get any better than this.

Moses and Dean celebrating their 50th wedding anniversary in Pennsylvania Amish Country.

Moses and Dean celebrating, just enjoying themselves in Oahu, Hawaii.

"Go Dean" with that mustang convertible in Hawaii!

Just hanging out and enjoying ourselves in Hawaii.

It's Hawaii, but it's cool today.

Moses' 75th birthday party. Even older people like a party with presents.

Even great-grandchildren: Raven (left) and little Adison (center) can teach Papa something new.

These children are such a blessing to us. They live next door across the road.

Great-grandson, Chase

Great-granddaughter, Raven

Great-granddaughter, Adison

Papa, let's build a bonfire. Raven, Adison, and Papa.

Left: Riding the scooters is real fun with Papa.

Moses, Chase, and Raven

Mema Dean and Papa Moses with the great-grandchildren enjoying the pool at the condo in Myrtle Beach.

Papa Moses and the girls building a sand castle at the beach.

Left: Moses "Gregg" King
Son of Moses and Dean King

Below: (L to R) Kallen,
Spencer, Scott, and Gregg.
"We are the family".

Moses and Dean's Daughter: Deborah "Debbie" Dean King

Moses and Dean's Daughter: Janet Carol King

"Good Memories"

Outdated poultry barn built in 1958 by Moses is now used for storage.
This was one of four laying houses used to produce hatching eggs in the 1960s and 1970s.

The farm office and garage are the center of today's "highly mechanized" farming operation.

The grain elevator stands ready to receive grain from the fields.

Our son, Gregg, posing beside the Rootster. This machine removes roots and stones from the soil.

Scott, our oldest grandson (standing), assisting his father, Gregg (in tractor), with some equipment adjustments.

Gregg poses with his equipment, ready to go to work.

Gregg relaxing with his Jack Russell "Sugar" after a long day's work.

Lean not to your own understanding,
but trust also in Me
and I will direct thy paths.

Proverbs 3:5, 6

Thy word is a lamp unto my feet, and a
light unto my path.

Psalm 119:105

The Holy Spirit is always faithful to direct us as we place our trust in His Word. On the following pages I have shared some paths that the Holy Spirit has guided me down by the scriptures. Each caption represents a different path in my personal pursuit of wisdom for my life's journey.

Please note as you read this section that the words of Jesus himself are used over and over again regarding the first and second commandment, to shed light on our paths. May you sense the Holy Spirit speaking to you as you read, and be blessed.

–Moses King

SECTION
3

A Time of Reflection

Moses King

SECTION 3

A Time of Reflection

As I look back at the open door God placed before us in 2004 regarding kingdom giving, I can't help but remember the prophetic words that I received earlier that same year. Kingdom giving is always an open door. Christians receive insight and inspiration from the Holy Spirit concerning needs. The Holy Spirit then illuminates our minds with a divine strategy. We then choose to walk through that open door, or we choose to decline that opportunity.

What God was leading us into was a large commitment—larger, in fact, than I had ever known an individual to undertake. We planned to contribute $250,000 per year for five years, creating a $1 million endowment and a $250,000 gift fund. Not only was it a large commitment over five years, but the Holy Spirit also gave directions on how these funds should be invested and spent to accomplish His purpose. Let us look again at these earlier prophetic words so we can see the Holy Spirit at work:

1. Look back and acknowledge that God has been with you in the past.
2. There will be miracles of directions.
3. I will give miracles of conquest over permanents.[1]
4. I will give miracles of provision with what you already have.

As we moved forward to accomplish what God had birthed in our spirit, we felt such a sense of excitement in watching God perform miracles of provision with what we already had. I'm reminded of several times in the Bible when God would use whatever an individual had in his or her hand whenever that person encountered God. Moses used his rod many times to do mighty things. Samson used the jawbone of an ass to slay a mighty troop. David used his shepherd's sling and a smooth stone from the brook to slay Goliath. The

---

1. The word "permanents" for King refers to those things the world considers to be "permanent," but that in light of eternity are transient and thus are such that the miraculous power of God can change them.

widow used her oil in obedience to a word from God's servant, Elisha, and always had enough for herself, her son, and Elisha during famine.

We know that in God's kingdom the supernatural is a normal process because it's God's kingdom. These examples of divine intervention or the supernatural coming into the domain of the human experience are from the Old Testament, and they illustrate that God has *always* visited his people in tangible ways.

In the New Testament, Jesus came to redeem us. He also came to empower us for living in this world in the dispensation of grace. While He dwelt among us, He taught us through His words and deeds. When He returned to the Father to sit at His right hand, He sent the Holy Spirit to remind us of all He had said and done.

Jesus also taught us to pray to our Father in heaven that His kingdom come on earth as it is in heaven. Why? How? Is His kingdom only abiding in us as the Scripture speaks about, or can we reason that He really meant what He had prayed?

"Thy kingdom come, Thy will be done in earth, as it is in heaven," resonates in my spirit. Could it be that Jesus gave us the keys to His kingdom on the earth, but we failed to understand what He taught us? It seems to me that spiritually our Lord was prophetically telling us that His kingdom has always been at work; therefore, "Look back and acknowledge that God has been with you in the past."

As I reflect over the last two decades, I am drawn to two special encounters with miracles of provision and guidance. I shared earlier in this book the significance of what I learned from the Holy Spirit concerning Jesus' teaching about the first and second commandments. What are we to learn from these special encounters? Why are other people (our neighbors) so important in our relationships in kingdom living? Let's look at another parable that Jesus taught us concerning a treasure hidden in the field.

THE TREASURE (GOD'S KINGDOM) IS IN THE FIELD OF SERVING OTHERS.

We must love our neighbors as ourselves as we travel through this world if we are to obtain this treasure. When Jesus was asked about which commandment was the greatest, he replied that the first commandment was, "love the Lord thy God with all thy heart, and with all thy soul, and with all thy mind," and "the second is like unto it, Thou shalt love thy neighbor as thyself. On these two commandments hang all the law and the prophets" (Matthew 22:37-40).

Over and over in Scripture we are reminded that Christian service is all about giving of ourselves to others (our neighbors), just as Jesus gave Himself for us as our Savior and Redeemer. Just as Jesus abandoned His will for the will of God the Father, we are encouraged to sell or abandon our selfishness and self-indulgence so that we may buy the field which contains the treasure of great value (Matthew 13:44).

Jesus said that the field was the world. Jesus also taught us in scripture that the kingdom of heaven is the treasure of great value. Is Jesus not, then, teaching us in the Lord's Prayer to pray for the kingdom of God to be realized in our life experiences as we work in the field of Christian service in this world? Is the secret in this parable not the same as the truth revealed by Jesus in His answer regarding the greatest commandment? First, we are to love God; second, we are to validate our relationship with God through Jesus Christ by "selling" or abandoning our self-interests and serving others with the same commitment that we have to ourselves.

How do we enter into the field of service? It's helpful to understand that in this world Christians who have "sold out for Jesus," or have abandoned their selfishness for the love of Christ, are a part of the body of Christ. Therefore, we have abandoned our selfishness to unite with Christ and his body (church) to carry out the Great Commission. When we are united with other believers of like faith, we have positioned ourselves for maximum impact in the world or the field. It is there that the treasure of great value, "Thy kingdom come … in earth as it is in heaven," is more likely to be realized, as we submit to the leading of the Holy Spirit and totally commit ourselves to God's will for the benefit of others (our neighbors).

As Paul proclaimed while sharing the gospel in Athens, as kingdom people we live, move and have our being in Christ Jesus, our Lord and King (Acts 17:28). We are His offspring, which means we have His spiritual DNA (17:29). As we live, move and have our being in Christ, the King of kings, we must be sensitive as part of his functioning body on earth (the church) to our role as both kings and priests. Do not all kingdoms have a king? How, then, can God's kingdom function in lives on this earth, as He taught us to pray, without the spiritual King in us? We must become mature and start functioning in divine authority! According to Paul in Acts 17:29, we are Christ's offspring; we have the DNA of the King of kings. Let us look for every opportunity to take dominion in this world through Jesus Christ, the King of all eternity. Amen and amen.

KINGS AND PRIESTS

In the book of Revelation, John wrote that the redeemed were made kings and priests through Jesus Christ unto God his Father (1:5, 6). Are we not, then, supposed to walk in these offices now, as we live and pray to our Heavenly Father, "Thy Kingdom come on earth"? What does it mean to walk or function in the office of a king or priest in God's kingdom on this earth? In Revelation 1:7 John writes about Christ coming in the clouds, so this leaves little doubt that if we are kings and priests in verse 6, He has reference to our functions in God's kingdom on the earth.

We have a broad understanding about the priestly calling of ministers to proclaim the good news of salvation; however, we lack understanding about walking in, or functioning in, the office of a king in God's kingdom on the earth. Why? Can it be that we have failed to recognize the church as the body of Christ on the earth today? The church is made up of mostly laity. We are told by the statisticians that the priestly gifting and calling in the body of Christ represents only one percent of the Christian church today. Yet Scripture tells us that within the body of Christ everyone has callings and gifts that are profitable for fulfilling the Great Commission to go into the entire world and make disciples.

In the case of those whom God by his Holy Spirit does not call into the priestly area of ministering the Word, they are often left in the body with the large perception that they are "just laymen." Furthermore, priestly leadership often affirms that the remaining members are indeed "just laymen," without an adequate understanding of who they are in Christ. It seems like a reasonable conclusion that if we are all kings and priests and God does not call us into the priestly ministry, then our "gifting and calling" must be as kings in God's kingdom on earth.

What, then, is our role as kings in Christ and kingdom living? What is our role as kings in Christ in fulfilling the Great Commission? We have some excellent examples in the Old Testament with King David and King Solomon. Both kings had a heart for God. Both kings had imperfections, but they were still used by God. It is very noteworthy that these men were not priests or ministers, but God used them mightily to serve His purposes.

King David is said to be a man after God's own heart (Acts 13:22). He was a warring king. He was zealous in conquering territories and taking dominion. King Solomon, on the other hand, was not a warring king, as his father, David, had been. He was a king of peace and prosperity. He built the temple of the Lord with great splendor and honor. Solomon prayed to God for wisdom to rule wisely, and God granted him great wisdom and prosperity (1 Kings 3:3-15; 6:1-38; 2 Chronicles 1:1–7:22).

What important roles does God want kings to fulfill in the body of Christ today? As we ponder this important question, let us agree that there is much diversity in the body of Christ. Just as David and Solomon were vastly different in their roles as kings, so is every member of the body of Christ different in callings and gifts. In our role as kings in the body of Christ today, are we not needed to take dominion like David over territories that have fallen to the kingdom of God by the preaching of the Word? We do that by building churches and Bible schools in those areas where the preaching of the gospel has broken down the strongholds of sin and evil.

Just like Solomon, we are to pray for wisdom to walk upright among men and to make wise choices that bring forth prosperity into the kingdom effort. This is a laity gifting that needs to be stirred up and called forth. Every member of the body of Christ has this gifting to varying degrees. Wisdom to make right choices is the children's bread. Could it be that the Holy Spirit is stirring up these kings in the body today for the latter day's harvest? Through Jesus Christ, are we not all kings and priests in God's kingdom on this earth? Yes, we are all kings and priests in God's kingdom on the earth as we faithfully keep the first and second commandments. Amen and amen!

MONEY AND GOD'S KINGDOM ON EARTH

Consider this: God does not need our money! As kings, however, we have a need to be vested in God's kingdom on the earth. Wouldn't it be rather ridiculous to think that God could need our money? God blessed us with these resources out of His abundance in heaven by His grace. The God of heaven owns everything. Does He not provide these resources so we can be a part of what He is doing on the earth today? He commands us to bring our tithes and offerings into the storehouse of the Lord. He gives us a benchmark for the tithe of ten percent to guide us in our giving. This doesn't mean that the ninety percent that is left after the tithe belongs to us, however.

The Bible teaches us that we are not our own, for we have been bought with the price of the shed blood of Jesus (Acts 20:28; 1 Corinthians 6:19, 20). If we truly understand that we belong to Jesus, as we have been redeemed by His shed blood, surely we should understand that the money and possessions that He has provided for our benefit and pleasure belong to the loving Heavenly Father also. Did He not provide it? How could we be so arrogant as to think that what the Lord has given belongs to us and still stand proudly on Sunday and sing "Amazing Grace"? Should we not be grateful and delighted that everything God has entrusted to our care belongs to the Creator God, who loved us so much as to send His own son, Jesus Christ, to redeem us to right relationship with Him? As the psalmist says, "Delight thyself also in the LORD; and he shall give thee the desires of thine heart" (Psalm 37:4).

JESUS MAKES "US" DIFFERENT

Jesus spoke a parable as He taught the people about a certain rich man whose grounds brought forth an abundant harvest (Luke 12). The response of the rich landowner was to pull down his barns and build bigger barns, which seemed like a prudent thing to do. His selfish response, however, reveals why God responded by calling him a fool or foolish man. Why would God take such a strong position against his decision to build bigger barns?

The answer is revealed in his statement, "I will say to my soul, 'Soul, thou hast much goods laid up for many years; take thine ease, eat, drink, and be merry'" (Luke 12:19). We see no recognition of God as the provider of this great harvest. The foolish man's self-centered attitude reflects the basic sin that so often besets the human experience as we journey through this world. The landowner was only focusing on himself and his own personal pleasures. Is it not this selfishness that is the taproot of all man's sin and disobedience? We who are the redeemed of the Lord through Jesus Christ must resist the thinking of this world system.

Jesus commands us, "Seek ye first the kingdom of God, and his righteousness; and all these things shall be added unto you" (Matthew 6:33). We have a new and better covenant through Jesus Christ, who has redeemed us from sin and the world system of selfishness. This new and better covenant was plainly revealed to us by Jesus when He was asked by the Pharisees which was the greatest commandment of all. Jesus replied, "Thou shalt love the Lord thy God with all thy heart, and with all thy soul, and with all thy mind ... And the second is like unto it, Thou shalt love thy neighbor as thyself. On these two commandments hang all the law and the prophets" (Matthew 22:36-40).

We see in Jesus' own words that we have a simple mandate to love God first and to love others as we love ourselves. This lays the ax to the taproot of selfishness and prepares us for kingdom living as we walk in love among others. Could it be that when Jesus taught us to pray, "Thy kingdom come. Thy will be done in earth as it is in heaven," that He had more in His mind for us than we have grasped? The first commandment speaks of the total commitment that we are to bring to Jesus. We are to put Him first. The second commandment provides us with a tangible way of verifying that the taproot of selfishness has been rooted up and dealt with by faith in Jesus Christ.

Could it be that, even now, we allow small vestiges of selfishness to live quietly below the surface in our relationships with others (our neighbors)? Sometimes, we may not be aware of the problem, since this is normal thinking for the world system that surrounds us. This could be compared to a light infestation of termites in a building. The damage is done out of sight, always quietly and unknown to the property owner. Could it be that this subtle condition could be hindering the supernatural flow of kingdom blessings to the redeemed?

Dear Jesus, as you have taught us to pray, "Thy kingdom come ... in earth as it is in heaven," please wash away every vestige of selfishness (both known and unknown) from our hearts, that we might enjoy God's kingdom on this earth. Amen.

I WILL DIRECT THY PATH

"Lean not to your own understanding, but trust also in me, and I will direct thy paths." These words from Proverbs 3:5, 6 give us tremendous insight into kingdom living in our personal, day-to-day life experiences. Do these verses *not* lead us to experience the kingdom of God on the earth in such a way that allows us to access His resources in heaven? As we walk with God in this world, we walk many paths that are winding and uphill. Seldom have we reached the top of any mountain without traveling this type of winding path, with many blind curves and steep inclines. Then finally, we break out into the glorious sunlight and we are able to view the splendor of God's handiwork on a higher plain.

On our journey to the mountaintop, we have to be focused on staying on the *right side* of this winding road and trusting in God's care to keep us. Is it not the same with our spiritual journey? We often lack understanding because we haven't been this way before. As we travel the winding paths of our human experience, the most fundamental principal of God's word is that we always stay focused on *doing what is right*. We are sometimes tempted to cross over the line just a little and yield to the thinking of this world's system. Then the prompting of God's spirit will beckon to us and remind us that in God's kingdom the *words of the King* are where kingdom authority exists. Whatever Jesus taught us in his word is where the children of the King will find their greatest delight, comfort and strength.

> Delight thyself also in the LORD; and he shall give thee the desires of thine heart. Commit thy way unto the LORD; trust also in him; and he shall bring it to pass. ... The steps of a good man are ordered by the LORD: and he delighteth in his way. Though he fall, he shall not be utterly cast down: for the LORD upholdeth him with his hand (Psalm 37:4, 5, 23, 24).

Psalm 37:24 suggests that even when we are walking in a delighted relationship with the King, we may come under attack by our adversary, Satan. If we are walking in the love of God and serving the King of kings with great pleasure and delight, then how can this be? If we are walking with God with great commitment, how can Satan have access to us? Are we not kingdom people, walking in obedience to the kingdom principles of God's word? How does Satan attack us when we are walking close to God, when we are walking in obedience to kingdom principles?

Although we are faithfully doing whatever God has called us to do, we are still living in a sin-tossed world. Does not the story of Job give us some insight into what kind of devices Satan chooses to use against those who stand faithfully before God day by day, refusing to give up in this battle against sinful domination of our human experience? God was proud of his servant, Job. Job walked upright before God. Satan, then, with God's permission, chose to attack Job by attacking his children and destroying Job's most prized reason for living.

Have we not seen Satan use such devices against God's chosen servants in our generation? We the redeemed of the Lord Jesus Christ sometimes come under this attack of Satan against our families. Satan comes forth to steal, kill and destroy. Sometimes Satan's evil devices cause the complete loss of our children in death. Sometimes Satan attacks our children in other devious ways to cause our children and us much pain and heartache. Does this indicate that we are not in a right relationship with God? Consider again the story of Job for the correct answer to this age-old question.

Sometimes Satan will try to hinder God's children by attacking them in their finances. Look at Job for an illustration of Satan's devious ways in this area. Consider again the characteristics of Satan and his devices. Satan comes forth to steal, kill and destroy. After he had killed or stolen away all of Job's children and possessions (Job 1:13-22), he finally got permission from God to touch Job's very body and inflict both physical and mental pain upon him (Job 2:1-10).

There are also times in our human experiences when our friends, both inside and outside the church, will turn on us to devour our joy. They will accuse us unjustly before God and man. Such a heinous attack straight from the pits of Hell is often intended to be Satan's knockout blow because it challenges our very relationship with God. The Bible tells us that Satan is the accuser of the brethren. He will often use someone close to us as his mouthpiece. Does this mean that we are out of a proper relationship with God? Here again, it's helpful to look to the story of Job for the correct answer.

Also in Psalm 37:24, we are given two important lessons about kingdom living, both of which are vital for us to grasp and hold on to, as kingdom Christians. First, we understand that our adversary, Satan himself, may attack us in some sneaky way, even while we are walking upright with God in a kingdom relationship. Second, the good news in this verse is that if we are cast down by life's circumstances or Satan's attacks, we have God's promise that he is holding us with his hand, to lift us up by his strong arm. God is the lifter of our heads in all circumstances. It is also helpful to remember that we are still living in a sin-dominated world. We are blessed also to know that God wants to direct our paths, if we will only trust in him instead of our own selfish (world system) thinking.

LET EVERY MAN JUDGE HIMSELF

How can we know when we are putting God first and trusting in Jesus' words instead of our own selfish thinking? For a correct answer to this question, we would be well advised to look again to Scripture for insight. The best illustration is given by Jesus in His answer to the Pharisees in Matthew's Gospel. Consider the words of Jesus in these verses:

> Then one of them, which was a lawyer, asked him a question, tempting him, and saying, Master, which is the great commandment in the law? Jesus said unto him, Thou shalt love the Lord thy God with all thy heart, and with all thy soul, and with all thy mind. This is the first and great commandment. And the second is like unto it. Thou shalt love thy neighbor as thyself. On these two commandments hang all the law and the prophets (Matthew 23:35-40).

In the second commandment, Jesus gives us a self-test formula to help us judge our own hearts and our propensity toward selfishness. Would Jesus have taught us to pray, "Thy kingdom come. Thy will be done in earth, as it is in heaven," without it being in our realm of possibility? Why is it so important to love our neighbors as ourselves? We have good understanding about the first commandment, while we often ignore the second commandment, thinking it irrelevant to us as Christians in this dispensation of grace.

Often when we are confronted with kingdom teaching, we will then rush to the truth that the kingdom of God is within us, since the Holy Spirit dwells in us. Is this all Jesus had in mind when he taught us to pray, "Thy kingdom come. Thy will be done in earth, as it is in heaven"? Do you not agree that the love of God or the kingdom of God in our lives is supposed to be manifest in our relationship with our neighbors or others, as Jesus taught us in the second commandment? Only this truly validates to God and man that we are kingdom people. Only this type of relationship with others as we encounter them throughout our lives attests to our kingdom relationship with God through Jesus Christ.

Let's look at another parable that Jesus taught: "Again, the kingdom of heaven is like unto treasure hid in a field; the which when a man hath found, he hideth, and for joy thereof goeth and selleth all that he hath, and buyeth that field" (Matthew 13:44). The treasure of God's kingdom is in the field of unselfishness. We must abandon our selfishness and self-indulgence in exchange for the field of service to others in order to obtain this treasure of great price.

We cannot buy the treasure, but we can buy the field that contains the treasure. We cannot buy the field that contains the treasure with money. We can only obtain this kingdom relationship by first giving ourselves unreservedly to God and then by loving our neighbors as ourselves in unselfish consideration for others. Could it be that only in this field does the kingdom of heaven flow into our tangible human experiences on this earth?

Could it be that only in this field does the kingdom of heaven flow into our tangible human experiences on this earth?

Jesus says that the field is white unto harvest, and "he that reapeth receiveth wages, and gathereth fruit unto life eternal" (John 4:35, 36). WOW! Jesus also says the treasure is in the field. Is not the treasure of great price God's kingdom in this present world? "Thy kingdom come. Thy will be done in earth, as it is in heaven." So, when we give of ourselves in Jesus' name, we are fulfilling the second commandment, and we are working in the field. We are positioning ourselves to enjoy the blessings of kingdom living. *When God's kingdom comes to us on earth, the supernatural is released to us on earth to accomplish natural things.* This amazes us, but in God's kingdom, God's power is empowering our natural ability to accomplish the things we need to accomplish. WOW! God's kingdom on earth has the same power that exists in God's kingdom in heaven. Therefore, we pray in faith as Jesus taught us to pray, "Thy kingdom come. Thy will be done in earth as it is in heaven."

Jesus said of himself in John 10:10, "I am come that they might have life, and that they might have it more abundantly." As we confess Jesus Christ as the Son of God and repent of our sins, we become kingdom people spiritually. Should we not, in our human experience as kingdom people on earth, move out into the fields by serving our neighbors as Jesus taught? Then, should we not claim the abundant life that Jesus has provided for us in the tangible arena of our lives also? Should we not pray, "Thy kingdom come. Thy will be done in earth as it is in heaven"? Should we not expect God to answer that prayer by directing his power to flow into our unselfish tangible circumstances to produce in us the abundant life that Jesus has provided for us?

Thy kingdom come. Thy will be done in earth, as it is in heaven! Amen.

THE STRUGGLES OF LIFE

As I was traveling down the path of life back in 1992, I was faced with many twists and turns that easily could have overwhelmed me. As I prayed month after month and sought God for wisdom and direction, the word of God broke forth into my presence. As I waited before the Lord, a voice of divine origin spoke these words of scripture into my life with divine authority: "Lean not to your own understanding, but trust also in me, and I will direct thy path."

Sometimes divine encounters are misunderstood when one makes an effort to share them with others. As I have stated earlier, this was a life-changing event for me. As I sought to follow the King of kings more fully, I began to understand more clearly that the redeemed are indeed all kings and priests in God's kingdom on earth. Just as Jesus is our Great High Priest and King of kings, so also are we all kings and priests in God's kingdom on earth through Jesus Christ. We have inherited His DNA through redemption by His shed blood. We also have gifts and callings for kingdom living and kingdom work. Just like ants in their respective colonies, every redeemed person should understand that in the domain of God's kingdom on earth, there is a unique place and a unique gifting for every person.

It is my prayer that a mighty army of believers will be enlightened and encouraged in their understanding regarding laymen (kings) in the kingdom of God on the earth. Is it not time that the church of Jesus Christ lift up, motivate and call forth this mighty army of believers whom we call laymen, as we teach them how important the kingship of believers in Christ really is? There are no indications in Scripture that those who are not of the priestly order as ministers of the gospel will be presented to God as laymen. Jesus himself will present us all to God the Father as "kings and priests" (Revelation 1:6). This is true in a spiritual sense because we have Christ's spiritual DNA.

Accordingly, if we are to pray, "Thy kingdom come. Thy will be done in earth, as it is in heaven," then we as the body of Christ should reflect His nature and characteristics as we go about life in His earthly kingdom. America and the world at large will be impacted greatly by God's kingdom on earth if we can encourage and mobilize the laity of the church.

This ninety-nine percent of the body of Christ represents the financial and service sector of God's kingdom on the earth. The laity (kings) has all the financial and manpower resources needed to carry out the Great Commission and the end-time harvest. It's up to the priestly leadership to lead the way to the cross and call forth by the Holy Spirit the financial resources needed in God's kingdom on earth.

God is presenting us with a new paradigm regarding kingdom realities and the ministries of His church. The old paradigm or way of thinking must be challenged if we are to improve our effectiveness in ministry. A preacher and his board with a church full of others who are "just laymen" leave most of Christ's church feeling of little importance or significance.

In Genesis we see Melchizedek, our first type of Christ in the Old Testament, who was both king of Salem (Jerusalem) and priest of the Most High God (14:18). Melchizedek brought forth bread and wine and served Abram. As priest of the Most High God, he also received tithes from Abram.

In the New Testament, Jesus Christ is hailed as King of kings and Lord of lords and our Great High Priest. Are we not all redeemed into union with Jesus Christ, who died for us? Are we not all one body fitly joined together, filled with His Spirit and sent forth in this world under His lordship? Our thinking and our ministry model, then, should more effectively project these realities of spiritual authority and power to the entire body of Christ, both kings and priests.

BEWARE OF HUMANISM
(SATAN'S COUNTERFEIT CHRISTIANITY)

When humanity chooses to bypass Jesus' first commandment and build their approach to God on the second, Satan certainly must rejoice. The selfish human spirit can easily be convinced that meeting others' needs through Christian service as Jesus taught will surely gain them eternal life. However, by Jesus' own words to Nicodemus, we are told that to inherit eternal life "[we] must be born again" (John 3:7).

Regardless of how much money we give to the church or how much Christian service we perform, we still must come to God through the first commandment to inherit eternal life. The story of the rich young ruler is placed in Scripture to dispel all questions about our ability to work our way into redemptive grace. We cannot bypass the first and greatest commandment of all.

Why, then, is the second commandment to love our neighbors as ourselves so important? Could it be that fulfilling the second commandment is our key to releasing the blessings of kingdom living into our personal life experiences on this earth? "Thy kingdom come. Thy will be done in earth, as it is in heaven." Amen and amen!

THE REST OF THE STORY

God began stirring my spirit concerning the role of laymen in the body of Christ in the early 1980s. Later in the 1980s, an anonymous minister preaching on Christian radio planted in my life the reality that we are all kings and priests in God's kingdom.

As I was driving to the office one day, I was scanning the Christian radio stations for something of interest when I stumbled into this sermon already in progress. The minister was eloquent in his proclamation that we were all kings and priests in God's kingdom on this earth. He spoke of the importance of recognizing our kingly role, just as others recognize their priestly call. If Jesus is going to present us as kings and priests to the Father (Revelation 1:6), then we are kings and priests now as His redeemed. Only our calling and gifts are different, according to God's purpose for our lives.

That insight was such an encouragement to me as a layman. This truth began to connect with the unrest that was already in my spirit concerning the role of the laity in the body of Christ. I believe that we are moving into a dispensation when God is calling laymen forth to come alongside those with a priestly calling for the great last days of harvest.

In my heart I sense that the "rest of the story" is still being written as godly men and women embrace these truths from God's Word. It is time for the church of Jesus Christ to arise, all of us together, to do our part in our generation so that "His will" be done on earth as it is in Heaven!

Bangladesh

Rangpur

INDIA

Brahmaputra

Mymensingh

Sylhet

Jamuna

Rājshāhi

Ganges

Tungi

DHAKA

Nārāyanganj

Comilla

Meghna

Jessore

Khulna

Barisāl

Mongla

Chittagong

Keokradang

Mouths of the Ganges

...land

Cox's
Bāzār

Bay of Bengal

Vijay and Apa Balla with Scott and Brandi King at the dedication of the new school in Bangladesh.

King family in Bangladesh. L to R: Retired missionary Joe Arthur, missionary Russell Board (continential director, Asia/Australia), Scott and Brandi King, and missionaries Dr. and Mrs. Vijay Balla.

Turkey

Black Sea

RUS

G

Zonguldak

lapazari

Trabzon

Ankara

Sivas

Erzurum

hya

TURKEY

Elâzig

Malatya

Diya

Maras

Adana

Tarsus

Antalya

Mersin

CYP.

SYRIA

Sea

Beirut

LEB.

40°

Moses and Dean near Hierapolis (Colossians 4:13), modern Pamukkale, Turkey.

Ruins of Biblical Laodicea. The King family contributed to the IPH church plant near here.

Dean at Ephesus archaeological site.

Pastor Ismail Serinken, leader of IPHC Turkey.

And he said unto them, Go ye into all the world, and preach the gospel to every creature.

Mark 16:15 (KJV)

OUR TRAVELS
Hungary & Ukraine

Doug Beacham and Moses King with translator, Dr. Sergey Perkhalsky, speaking in Kiev, Ukraine.

Moses King sharing with a men's group in Ukraine.

The late IPHC missionary David Fannin, Valery Alymov, Moses King, Doug Beacham, and Dr. Sergey Perkhalsky.

The late David Fannin, Bob Cave (WMM continental director for Europe/Middle East), Doug Beacham, and Moses King share a meal with a Ukrainian family in the village of Volytsya, where an IPH church has been established.

Doug Beacham, Moses King, Pastor Joseph Gere and his wife, Lilia,
in Szigetszentmiklos, near Budapest, Hungary.

David Fannin, Moses King, Doug Beacham, Senior Pastor Reshetinsky of Christian Hope Church,
local pastors, and Bob Cave in Kiev, Ukraine.